C·H·I·C·K·E·N
S·A·L·A·D·S

C·H·I·C·K·E·N
S·A·L·A·D·S

*60 Scrumptious Recipes for an
American Classic*

Carole Lalli

📖 HarperPerennial
A Division of HarperCollins*Publishers*

HarperCollins books may be purchased for educational, business, or sales promotional use. For information please write: Special Markets Department, HarperCollins Publishers, Inc., 10 East 53rd Street, New York, NY 10022.

FIRST EDITION

Designed by Stephanie Tevonian

Library of Congress Cataloging-in-Publication Data

Lalli, Carole, 1942–
    Chicken salads : 60 scrumptious recipes for an American classic / by Carole Lalli.
        p. cm
    ISBN 0-06-095062-5
    1. Cookery (Chicken). 2. Cookery, American. 3. Salads. I. Title.
    TX750.5.C45L35 1994
    641.6'65—dc20   93-44625

94 95 96 97 98 ❖/RRD 10 9 8 7 6 5 4 3 2 1

C·O·N·T·E·N·T·S

A·C·K·N·O·W·L·E·D·G·M·E·N·T·S

Thanks to the butchers at Kircher's Colonial Meat Market for the almost daily speedy delivery of many, many chickens and no questions asked.

I also want to acknowledge the authors whose recipes provided the inspiration for some of mine: Sarah Belk, Michael McCarty, Julia Child, Giuliano Bugialli, Johanne Killeen and George Germon, Perla Meyers, Zarela Martinez, Ken Hom, Molly O'Neill, Wolfgang Puck, and Michael McLaughlin.

I·N·T·R·O·D·U·C·T·I·O·N

Introduction

Buying Chicken

Cleaning and Storing Chicken at Home

Chicken Safety

Introduction

Poultry is for the cook what canvas is for the painter.
—Jean Anthelme Brillat-Savarin
Let's face it, chicken goes with anything.
—Frank Lalli, August 1993

||||||||||||||||||||||||||||||||||||||||||||||||||||||||||||||||||||||||||||||||||||||||||||||||||||||||||||||||||||

Deep into the testing of recipes for this book, the renowned versatility of chicken took on new meaning. Having accepted my publisher's challenge to create a chicken salad for every week of the year, I then experienced some doubts. It sounded like an awful lot of chicken salad. But once the process was underway, the possibilities were nearly limitless, especially nowadays when the concept of chicken salad has been stretched to include just about any combination of chicken—cooked by any known method—and other ingredients.

"Chicken salad" once meant leftovers from Sunday's roast chicken, heavily mayonnaised, with perhaps a bit of celery thrown in to add texture and some, but not too much, interest. Today's chicken salad has evolved from that model and is much more than a filling for sandwiches and hollowed-out tomatoes. It is practically emblematic of the startlingly cosmopolitan nature of today's American home cooking. Once the cooking of France and Italy became at least passingly familiar, Asian, Mexican, and Caribbean styles, among others, easily made their impact on the American pantry and on the family dining table. Flavors and ingredients that no longer seem very "foreign" have expanded the style and range of chicken salad. Reacquainting ourselves with some of our own regional cooking, such as Cajun and Southwestern, also increased the possibilities.

Chicken salad not only addresses the demands of the national palate but the issue of fat in food, today's most compelling food-related health concern. As more and more Americans eat less and less red meat, chicken consumption continues to rise. The drift from animal fat also has led to an increase in the use of olive and other oils. Egg-rich mayonnaise may once have been the dressing of choice for chicken salad, but many of the recipes here are oil-based. And there are some that use little fat of any kind, such as those with a tomato-based vinaigrette and the ones inspired by Asian dishes. In addition, these recipes reflect the growing interest in beans, grains, and vegetables; pasta, by now a staple of the American larder, is included in quite a few.

Finally, today's cook not only wants food that tastes good and is good for us, but that is relatively quick and easy to prepare. Many of the chicken salads in this book are, in fact, one-dish meals. As such, they may have as many components as any meal, but most of them can be prepared or partially prepared in advance and served cold or at room temperature. This makes them especially attractive for casual entertaining; many can be made in larger quantities than those given and served as parts of buffet parties.

Buying Chicken

With one exception, the recipes in this book call for either broiler-fryers or roasting chickens. The exception is a recipe for poussin or baby chicken, for which Cornish hens can be substituted.

Broiler-fryers weigh from 2 to 4 pounds. In fact, most of the chickens in our markets are mass-produced and rarely weigh under 3 pounds. A purely grain-fed or a free-range chicken may weigh around 2½ pounds.

Although a whole broiler-fryer can be roasted, a true roaster weighs more, from 4 to 8 pounds. In my experience, most of them are 6 to 7½ pounds, which is a good size for 4 to 6 servings.

FREE-RANGE, MASS-PRODUCED, AND KOSHER

A free-range chicken is, supposedly, one that has roamed and foraged for food in a barnyard. These chickens can be very good, and they also can be thin and tough. It all depends on what and how much was available for the birds to eat. If your goal is to avoid chickens that have been raised on a lot of chemicals, look for grain-fed chickens, which are not necessarily free-range chickens. They exist, usually from fairly small, regional producers. Ask a good butcher about the poultry farms where you live.

Mass-produced chickens are said to be raised with more chemicals and more antibiotics than locally produced free-range or chemical-free chickens. Their food may not be grain or mostly grain. Many experts, however, believe that most big commercial growers put out a good, tasteful, consistent product.

Kosher chickens cannot have torn or bruised skin, which insures their greater freshness. They also are generally a week or two older than other types and they are salted, all of which makes for tastier meat. Sometimes, however, the salt does not bring out more chicken flavor so much as it adds the taste of salt, and some find the saltiness of kosher chicken excessive.

If you live near Chinese or other ethnic markets, you may want to explore the chicken possibilities there. One advantage will be that the birds might still have their heads, which will help you determine freshness—like fish, chickens are clear and bright-eyed when fresh. These chickens may also have their feet, which add flavor to broth and soup.

Cleaning and Storing Chicken at Home

It is hard to know how long a chicken has been in your market, and they do not always bear "sell by" dates. You should patronize a busy market that has high standards overall. I get most of my chickens from the butcher I've used for 13 years, and I know the brand of chicken he sells. A good, fresh chicken should keep in your refrigerator for up to two days.

It is a good idea to wash and clean a chicken as soon as you get it home, removing bloody bits or ends of blood vessels. Discard or separately store the neck and innards. Rinse the chicken well in cold water, dry it and rewrap in plastic wrap or a plastic bag, or put it in a covered dish. If you have bought a whole bird, stuff a couple of paper towels into the cavity to soak up bloody moisture.

I avoid freezing chicken because it does alter the flavor and texture, even after only a short time. Nevertheless, the advantages of having a chicken or two in the freezer are obvious, and certainly, if you do not use a fresh chicken within two days, you should freeze it. To freeze, clean the chicken as above, getting it as dry as possible, and then rewrap. I use plastic wrap or aluminum foil, *and* a tightly sealed plastic bag. Three or four months is the limit for frozen chicken. Remember, freezing slows the process of deterioration dramatically, but it does not stop it. If nothing else, freshness will be lost.

Chicken Safety

SALMONELLA

Salmonella is only one of numerous bacteria that can infect chickens and eggs as well as many other foods. But it is the association of salmonella with chicken and eggs that has caught our attention because of recent outbreaks in some parts of the United States and Great Britain. As bad as salmonella is—and it can be deadly—its prevention, and the prevention of other bacteria that can cause foodborne diseases, is quite simple.

♦ Thorough cooking destroys the salmonella bacteria. For chicken, the USDA recommends that chicken be cooked to an internal temperature of 180 degrees and boneless parts to 160 degrees, which may seem overcooked. In any case, taking the internal temperature of anything but a whole bird presents a challenge, so the general doneness test may be your best guide: The juices should run clear, with no trace of pink, when tested at the thickest part.

♦ The second important precaution is to clean up carefully after preparing chicken. That means that your work surface, your utensils, and your hands should get a good scrubbing, and don't forget to use a brush under your nails. Salmonella can easily be transferred to other foods; it also can infect you topically—a friend of mine developed a serious infection in her arm, apparently from salmonella that invaded a small cut on her finger.

It is by now well known that raw and undercooked eggs are also potential carriers of the salmonella bacteria. In fact, the recent outbreaks were first associated with eggs. To completely avoid the possibility of infection from eggs, only thoroughly cooked ones should be eaten.

Having said that, I will also say that our chicken and egg supply is safe overall, though the USDA cautions that any raw food of animal origin can be assumed to be contaminated. This obviously includes beef, pork, and other meats. It is worth remarking that while many people have eliminated soft-boiled eggs from their diets, they still take their hamburgers rare. And, there are many strains of salmonella, some far more virulent than others.

There are a few recipes in this book that call for raw eggs; one of them is the basic formula for mayonnaise, the base dressing for a number of the chicken salads. There is also a recipe for hard-yolk mayonnaise. Commercial mayonnaise, always a safe option, is a quite stable product whose high acidity can actually help prevent spoilage of the foods with which it is combined. So, the choice is yours. I occasionally use homemade mayonnaise (quite a lot of it during the testing for this book) and I sometimes serve a 4-minute egg to my young daughter. I buy my eggs and chickens from a butcher I've used for years, and he is as confident of his source as I suppose one can be. In short, the choice you make for yourself should be based on such factors as your age and general health, not to mention the potential anxiety you may suffer as a result of eating homemade mayonnaise.

SAFE PRACTICES

To avoid salmonella and other foodborne diseases, follow these practices:

♦ Wash hands well before and after handling food and utensils; use a fingernail brush.

♦ Keep raw chicken away from cooked foods and foods that are to be eaten raw; from surfaces, utensils, and serving dishes.

♦ When buying food, place poultry packages in plastic bags if possible to keep them out of contact with other groceries.

♦ Do not put cooked chicken back into a dish that held it before it was cooked unless you wash the dish well first.

♦ Do not reuse marinades.

♦ Thaw chicken in the refrigerator, in a microwave oven, or in cold water changed every 30 minutes—do not leave chicken out at room temperature to thaw.

♦ Cook chicken thoroughly as described in the discussion of salmonella on page 9.

♦ Do not interrupt cooking; for instance, if you are starting a dish in the oven and finishing it over charcoal, have your fire ready to receive the chicken directly from the oven.

♦ Do not cook at oven temperatures below 325 degrees.

♦ Do not taste raw or partially cooked chicken.

♦ Do not serve food at temperatures between 40 degrees and 140 degrees; this is the range in which most bacterial agents thrive.

♦ Refrigerate or freeze cooked chicken within 2 hours of serving, or just one hour if the day is hot.

♦ If in doubt, throw it out; the bacteria that cause foodborne illnesses do not necessarily look, taste, or smell differently than if unspoiled.

Throughout this book, I have suggested that marinated chicken be taken from the refrigerator 15 minutes or so before broiling or grilling. This has long been my practice, learned from chefs and cooking teachers who advise against cooking refrigerator-cold food, especially meats. I also sometimes leave foods at cool room temperature to marinate, especially if the marinade is highly acidic or spicy, although I do not suggest that in these recipes. Also, my own taste is for cool or room temperature rather than cold food and I believe that just about all the dishes in this collection will taste better at cool room temperature, not ice cold.

Clearly, these practices seem to fly in the face of the precautions, but the precautions themselves suggest that a little flexibility may be allowed. If, for instance, food can be kept out for 1 or 2 hours before being refrigerated, it surely will be somewhere in the "danger" zone of 40 degrees to 140 degrees. Conversely, a platter of chicken salad taken from the refrigerator, where the temperature generally hovers around 40 degrees, will similarly begin to climb into that zone immediately. You could gobble up the cold food of course, favoring food safety rules over the rules of etiquette. Or you can be careful all along the way, from the point of purchase to the point of dining, and make intelligent decisions about such issues as the exact temperature at which to serve food.

B·A·S·I·C
P·R·E·P·A·R·A·T·I·O·N·S
F·O·R C·H·I·C·K·E·N
S·A·L·A·D·S

Poaching
Roasting
Grilling and Broiling
Mayonnaise
Hard-boiled Egg Mayonnaise
Roasted Garlic

Poaching

Throughout this book, various preparations for the chicken are suggested. In some cases, considerable flexibility is indicated such as in recipes that call for grilled, broiled, or roasted chicken. In others, the preparation is far more specific. The more specific recipes frequently involve chicken that is first marinated and then grilled or broiled; in these, the marinade generally brings to the chicken some flavors that complement the other tastes in the salad.

However, part of the tradition of chicken salad is to use cooked chicken, often leftover, in another satisfying way. And one of the points of this book is to stretch the concept of chicken salad as a manageable, appealing, and certainly innovative dish. Therefore, even those seemingly specific recipes should be approached with the sense that alternative methods may work. For instance, I may suggest poached chicken for some dishes, but it is more than likely that roasted or grilled chicken will do just as well.

As to quantities, in most cases I have avoided giving very exact measures of the chicken to be used. For instance, quite a few recipes call for 3 whole chicken breasts, poached or grilled, with neither the weight nor cup measure indicated. This is based on my experience that the gross weight (on the bone) of 3 whole breasts is in the 3- to 3½-pound range, and that an ounce or two one way or the other is not going to have any real effect on the results. The 3 breasts are going to yield the 6 portions expected in the dishes calling for that amount, whether they are a touch larger or smaller than average. I think that when estimating servings of chicken, we tend to think in terms of pieces, rather than weights, per portion. For broiling and grilling, I generally have in mind a like size—3 to 3½ pounds, and for roasting, 6 to 7 pounds. These sizes fall into the ranges typically found in supermarkets and at butcher shops.

Chicken comes through the poaching process with more flavor if it is poached on the bone, with its skin still attached. It can be skinned, boned, and whole breasts can be separated after cooking. Skinless, boneless breasts can be used for the many recipes in this book that call for poached breasts; they will cook faster than chicken on the bone but might have less flavor. For the recipes in this book, herbs and other seasonings can be added to the poaching liquid, but it is not essential. All or some of the following can be used: small sliced onion, 1 or 2 cut-up carrots, bay leaf, thyme leaves, or parsley. The quantities of chicken specified relate to the amounts called for in most of the salad recipes.

1 to 2 cups homemade or commercial chicken broth
3 whole chicken breasts, 3 to 3½
pounds *or*

1 whole chicken, cut up, 3 to 3½
pounds

1. Pour the broth into a large shallow pan that will hold the chicken in 1 layer; a heavy sauté pan with a cover is ideal. Pour in enough water to cover the chicken by about ½ inch. Add any optional seasonings. Bring the liquid to a boil over medium high heat.

2. Add the chicken to the pan and more water if needed. Lower the heat to a simmer, cover the pan, and cook until the chicken is just cooked through. Breasts will take about 25 minutes (boneless breasts will need only about 20 minutes), while drumsticks will need about 30 minutes and thighs about 40. Remove the pan from the heat, uncover, and set aside for about 15 minutes before removing the chicken from the broth. Skin and bone the chicken and cut it up according to the salad you are preparing.

☛ **NOTE**: The poaching liquid can be strained and used as a base for soups or for poaching future chickens. Cool the broth, uncovered, at room temperature before storing it in the refrigerator or freezer. Chicken broth keeps well in the refrigerator for up to 1 week and for about 6 months in the freezer.

Roasting

METHOD #1—CONVENTIONAL OVEN

I roast my chickens in my conventional gas oven on high heat or in my covered kettle-type outdoor grill. If you have such a grill, I encourage you to begin cooking chicken this way; the results are truly superb. For any recipe in this book that specifies roasted chicken, or when any sort of cooked chicken is called for, a chicken roasted in a covered grill can be used.

1 large roasting chicken, 6 to 7 pounds
1 lemon, roughly cut up
1 head garlic, extra papery outside husk removed, and cut in half crosswise

Several twigs rosemary or thyme
1 tablespoon, more or less, olive oil

1. Preheat the oven to 450 degrees.

2. Wash and dry the chicken thoroughly. Stuff the cavity with the lemon, garlic, and herbs.

3. Rub the chicken all over with the olive oil. Place the chicken in a roasting pan (I use a 12-inch cast-iron skillet), on a rack if you wish, and place it in the preheated oven.

4. Roast, basting only once or twice, for 75 to 90 minutes. The chicken should be golden brown and crisp all over, and the juices running out of the thigh joint should be clear. The cooking time will vary, depending on the size of the chicken and the efficiency of the oven. Let the chicken rest for 15 minutes before cutting.

METHOD #2—COVERED GRILL

1. Prepare the chicken according to the directions for conventional roasting.

2. Place a disposable sheet pan about 9 inches by 12 inches or a double thickness of heavy duty foil in the center of the rack that holds the coals. Bank charcoal along the long sides of the pan or foil, up to the point of the grill rack. Prepare the fire. Or, first prepare your charcoal fire, then move the coals to the edges of the kettle and place the pan or foil in the center.

3. When the coals are ready, place the chicken in the center of the grill rack, over the drip pan. Cover the grill and open its vents. Roast the chicken for about an hour. Again, cooking times will vary, but this method can be quite rapid. Add coals if needed, though this is unlikely. Remove the chicken to a platter and let it rest for 15 minutes before cutting.

☛ **NOTE:** The chickens should not be trussed. They will cook faster and have crisper skin if the legs are left apart.

Grilling and Broiling

For chicken salads, I find it convenient to have the chicken split, but a quartered or cut-up bird can also be used. Many recipes throughout the book call for specific marinades. The flavorings used here are the ones I usually gravitate to for "generic" grilled chicken. Your own choices will do as well, but very specific flavors, such as soy sauce or hot spices, should be used only if they are compatible to the rest of the dish.

1 split broiler, 3 to 3½ pounds
Freshly squeezed juice of 1 lemon
3 or 4 garlic cloves, peeled and chopped
Leaves from 2 or 3 sprigs rosemary or thyme, or a mixture

Splash of red wine vinegar
1 to 2 tablespoons olive oil
Freshly ground black pepper

1. Place the chicken in a shallow glass or porcelain dish or in a zip-seal plastic bag.

2. Whisk the remaining ingredients together to combine well. Pour the marinade over the chicken or into the bag; be sure the chicken is coated all over. Cover the dish with plastic wrap or close the bag. Refrigerate the chicken for 4 hours or up to overnight.

3. Prepare a charcoal fire or preheat the broiler. Cook the chicken on both sides, starting skin side up, until well browned, crisp, and cooked through, about 20 to 25 minutes; the juices running from the thigh joint should be clear. Again, cooking times will vary with differences in the weight of the chicken and the fire or broiler.

Mayonnaise

||||||||||||||||||||||||||||||||||||||||||||||||||||||||||||||||||||||||||||||||||||||||||||||||||||||||||||||||||||||||||||||

Most of the recipes in this book that call for mayonnaise were tested with homemade or regular commercial mayonnaise as well as one or two of the leading "lower-fat" or "light" commercial types now on the market. Like everyone else, I have my personal favorite commercial mayonnaise, and, I suspect also like many others, it is the brand I grew up on. I truly cannot understand other preferences, but that's typical as well. For my taste, the lower-fat types were most successful in dressings that had other flavors going for them as well. The dressing for Chicken Salad Rémoulade, for instance, is enhanced with pickles, capers, herbs, and mustard; those assertive ingredients hide any textural or flavor weaknesses of reduced-fat mayonnaise.

The choice is yours. If you need to be or prefer to be on a fairly rigid low-fat regimen, you will want to continue, and by all means should use the lower-fat type whenever mayonnaise is called for. Others of us who monitor our fat intake on an ongoing basis can perhaps be more flexible and use homemade or regular commercial mayonnaise when the rest of our diets allow for that indulgence.

Mayonnaise is an emulsion sauce, which means that the oil is incorporated into the egg yolks and results in the familiar thick, creamy concoction that is perhaps the best-known sauce there is. For successful results, have your ingredients at room temperature and be very patient or the magic will not happen.

Mayonnaise also is a basic, codified sauce in that it depends on a fairly firm formula; there is a limit to how much oil can be emulsified with 1 egg yolk, and that limit ranges from ⅔ to ¾ cup. The difference relates to the size of the yolk. I always have "extra-large" eggs on hand and generally manage to incorporate ¾ cup of oil into 1 yolk.

Finally, for basic mayonnaise, I generally use half olive oil and half such neutral-flavored oil as safflower or soy. Peanut oils vary in depth of flavor; I recently used one that had an intense peanut taste, which is fine if that is the flavor you want in your sauce. Similarly, I do not generally use the most intensely rich extra-virgin olive oils when making mayonnaise. You should choose with the finished dish in mind. If you are making a Provençal or Italian dish with the mayonnaise, you may want to use more or even all olive oil and choose a richly flavored one. More delicate dishes may call for less than half olive oil in the mix.

✘ *Scant 2 cups*

2 egg yolks, at room temperature
1 tablespoon white or red wine
  vinegar
¼ teaspoon salt
½ teaspoon dry or prepared mustard (if prepared, Dijon or other not very harsh type)

¾ cup soy or safflower oil
¾ cup olive oil
2 tablespoons boiling water

1. In a medium-sized bowl, beat the yolks for 1 to 2 minutes, until they are quite thick and sticky.

2. Add the vinegar, salt, and mustard and beat to incorporate, about 30 seconds more.

3. While beating, add the oil, literally drop by drop, until the mixture begins to thicken and becomes creamy; this usually occurs when about ½ cup of oil has been used. The oil can now be added by the tablespoonful or in a thin, steady stream. If the sauce is thicker than you want it to be, add small amounts of vinegar or lemon juice to thin it; taste and add salt, freshly ground white or black pepper, or vinegar accordingly. Beat in the boiling water, which will help "hold" the sauce.

☛ **NOTE**: The recipe above is for mayonnaise made with a hand-held whisk or egg beater or an electric beater, fitted, preferably, with a balloon whisk attachment. To make the sauce in an electric blender, use a whole egg and 1 cup (total) of oil.

To make the sauce in a food processor, use 1 whole egg plus 1 yolk; you may need up to about ½ cup additional oil. Food processors tend to get warm and in turn may warm the mayonnaise, which can alter its flavor, as the egg cooks slightly.

☛ **HEALTH NOTE**: The problem of salmonella discussed on page 9 exists in raw eggs as well as undercooked chicken. If you want to avoid any possibility of salmonella, do not use homemade raw-egg mayonnaise.

Hard-boiled Egg Mayonnaise

✕ *1¼ cups*

3 hard-cooked egg yolks
1 tablespoon prepared Dijon mustard
¼ to ½ teaspoons salt

1 cup oil (half olive oil and half soy or safflower oil, or other combination)
Vinegar or lemon juice

1. Mash the yolks with the mustard and salt to taste in a mixing bowl until they become a completely smooth paste free of lumps.

2. Add the oil according to the directions for regular mayonnaise. Add vinegar or lemon juice to thin and season to taste.

Roasted Garlic

Roasted garlic is an ingredient in several recipes in this book. A head of garlic can easily be roasted in a conventional or microwave oven. I strongly suggest that to roast garlic you buy a terra cotta covered dish now available in stores and through mail-order catalogs. They come in sizes for just one or several heads of garlic. I use one frequently in my microwave oven. Any mention of a microwave oven makes some of my food-snob friends cringe, but it takes but a minute or so to produce a fragrant, tender head of roasted garlic.

1 unblemished head garlic	Salt and pepper
Sprig or two thyme or rosemary	1 teaspoon, more or less, olive oil

1. Preheat oven to 325 degrees.

2. Cut the top off the garlic to expose the flesh at the top of each clove. Remove the loose, papery outer leaves, but keep the head intact. Using a cake tester or other very fine pointed instrument, pierce the head in several places and set it in a small, deep dish. Sprinkle with the herbs, season to taste with salt and pepper, and drizzle the oil over. Cover the dish with a double thickness of aluminum foil and place in the oven. Remove the foil after 30 minutes. Bake for 15 or so additional minutes, until the cloves are tender; baste with additional small amounts of olive oil from time to time.

3. When the garlic is cool enough to handle, pinch the

cloves to release the roasted garlic, or use a tiny fork or knife point to pull the flesh from the cloves.

☛**NOTE**: To roast the garlic in a microwave oven, cover the dish with a saucer or plate and cook on high for 1 to 3 minutes. Take care; the garlic will toughen and dry out if it overcooks.

Mainly Chicken Salads

Chicken Salads with Vegetables

Chicken Salads with Pasta, Beans, and Grains

Mainly Chicken Salads

OLD-FASHIONED CHICKEN SALAD

T*his is the one to make for traditional chicken salad sandwiches, or to pile onto Bibb lettuce leaves, or to stuff into hollowed-out tomatoes. It will evoke memories of country club lunches with women wearing hats, even if that particular bit of nostalgia is outside your own experience.* ✕ *4 to 6 servings*

2 whole poached chicken breasts, boned, skinned, separated, and cut into small pieces

1 cup thinly sliced celery

1 tablespoon minced scallions

DRESSING
½ cup mayonnaise

2 tablespoons Dijon mustard

¼ cup heavy cream

2 tablespoons red wine vinegar

Salt

Freshly ground black or white pepper

1. Place the chicken, celery, and scallions in a medium-sized bowl.

2. Whisk together the ingredients for the dressing and pour it into the bowl. Toss to combine and season to taste with salt and freshly ground black or white pepper.

☛**NOTE:** One to two tablespoons fresh chopped herbs, such as chives, chervil, parsley, or tarragon can be added to the salad; chopped cucumbers can be substituted for the celery. To save the washing of a second bowl, mix the dressing in the bowl you will serve the salad in, then add the other ingredients.

CHICKEN SALAD BLT

⚔ *6 servings*

¼ pound slab bacon, cut into large dice

½ small head iceberg lettuce, cut into 1-inch pieces

2 whole poached chicken breasts, cut into 1-inch cubes

2 cups cherry tomatoes, cut in half

DRESSING

½ cup mayonnaise

1 tablespoon Dijon mustard

Few dashes Tabasco or similar hot pepper sauce

6 slices good-quality bread for toasting or grilling

1. Heat a medium-sized heavy skillet and add the bacon. Cook over medium-high heat, turning frequently, until it is browned and crisp all over and most of the fat has cooked off. Remove the bacon with a slotted spoon and drain on paper towels.

2. Whisk together the ingredients for the dressing.

3. When the bacon is cool, combine it in a bowl with the lettuce, chicken, and tomatoes. Add the dressing and toss to combine, taking care not to break up the tomatoes.

4. Toast or grill the bread; place the slices on individual plates and heap the salad on top; serve as open-faced sandwiches.

AUTUMN CHICKEN SALAD

✖ *8 to 10 servings as appetizer, 6 servings as entrée*

2 bunches watercress, trimmed, washed, and dried

3 whole poached chicken breasts, boned, skinned, and cubed, or 3½ to 4 cups roasted chicken, cubed

2 ripe pears (Bartlett, Bosc, Comice, or d'Anjou)

⅓ to ½ pound Gorgonzola or other best quality blue-veined cheese

DRESSING

1½ tablespoons drained green peppercorns in water

1 to 1½ tablespoons red wine vinegar

¾ cup walnut oil

Salt

Freshly ground black pepper

• • • • • • • • •

⅓ to ½ pound Gorgonzola or other best quality blue-veined cheese

¼ pound roughly chopped shelled walnuts, toasted

1. Place the watercress in a serving bowl or deep platter.

2. Place the chicken in a large mixing bowl. Peel and core the pears and cut them into 6 to 8 wedges, then cut the wedges in half crosswise. Add them to the bowl with the chicken.

3. Smash the peppercorns roughly with a small mortar and pestle or with the side of a spoon. Combine the peppercorns with the other dressing ingredients and whisk to blend well. Season with salt and freshly ground black pepper.

4. Pour some of the dressing over the watercress and toss. Pour additional dressing over the chicken and pears and toss gently; take care not to break the pear pieces. (You may not need all the dressing.)

5. Spoon the chicken mixture over the watercress. Crumble the cheese over the chicken and pears and toss the walnut pieces over all.

SARAH BELK'S CHICKEN SALAD WITH LEMON-CHIVE "BOILED" DRESSING

In *Belk's book,* **Around the Southern Table,** *much of the region's traditional cooking is reinterpreted and reinvented for modern cooks. This salad comes out of a long tradition: Chicken salads have been popular in the South, Sarah says, at least since Thomas Jefferson popularized salmagundi, a cold dish of chopped ingredients, and "boiled" dressings preceded the wide availability of good oils and vinegars and prepared dressings. In her version, Belk reduces the traditional vinegar and freshens the flavor with lemon juice.*
✗ *4 to 6 servings*

DRESSING
¼ cup white wine vinegar
¼ cup freshly squeezed lemon juice
⅛ teaspoon salt
½ cup heavy cream
1 large egg, well beaten
1 tablespoon chopped fresh chives
1 tablespoon chopped fresh tarragon
6 cups diced cooked chicken

1 to 2 tablespoons fresh chives, cut into 1-inch lengths (optional)
1 to 2 tablespoons fresh tarragon leaves (optional)
2 to 3 teaspoons grated lemon zest (optional)
4 cups trimmed watercress, washed and dried
4 cups Belgian endive or trimmed Bibb or Boston lettuce, washed and dried

1. To make the dressing, bring the vinegar, lemon juice, and salt to a boil in a medium saucepan. Reduce the heat to low. Add the cream, then the egg. Cook over low heat, stirring constantly, for 2 to 5 minutes, or until the mixture thickens and coats the back of a wooden spoon. Do not let the mixture overheat or it will curdle. Add the chives and tarragon and cool to room temperature.

2. Place the chicken in a bowl and toss it with ½ to ⅔ cup of the dressing, or enough to coat the chicken lightly. Taste, adding salt and pepper, and herbs to taste, if you are using them.

3. Line a platter or individual plates with the watercress and endive or lettuce leaves. Mound the chicken salad on top and garnish with the remaining herbs and lemon zest, if you like. Serve cool (not cold) or at room temperature and pass any remaining dressing at the table.

☞**NOTE**: The dressing can be kept, covered, in the refrigerator for up to 2 weeks. Sliced tomatoes, chopped bell peppers, diced celery, or hard-boiled eggs can be added to the chicken.

PESTO CHICKEN SALAD

✗ *6 to 8 servings*

3 whole poached chicken breasts, cubed, or about 5 cups cubed roasted chicken

⅓ cup pignolias (pine nuts), lightly toasted

3 medium ripe tomatoes, cut into wedges (optional)

DRESSING
1 cup basil leaves
½ cup Italian parsley leaves
½ cup extra-virgin olive oil
3 tablespoons mayonnaise
1 teaspoon red wine vinegar
Salt
Freshly ground pepper

1. Place the chicken in a serving dish.

2. Place the ingredients for the dressing in the work bowl of a food processor and process to blend well. Season with salt and freshly ground pepper; add additional vinegar if needed.

3. Combine the dressing with the chicken; sprinkle the pignolias over all and garnish with the tomatoes, if you like.

NEW AMERICAN CHICKEN SALAD

✕ *8 servings*

8 poussin (baby chickens) or
  Cornish hens, butterflied
12 ounces fresh goat cheese
6 scallions, trimmed and roughly
  cut up
6 tablespoons extra-virgin olive oil
2 teaspoons red wine vinegar
2 garlic cloves, peeled
1 cup loosely packed basil leaves
Salt
Freshly ground black pepper
Juice of 2 lemons

DRESSING
1 large very ripe tomato, peeled,
  seeded, and cut into large
  chunks
6 to 8 tablespoons extra-virgin
  olive oil
2 teaspoons red wine vinegar

•   •   •   •   •   •   •   •   •   •

6 cups mixed lettuces, such as
  salad bowl, Bibb, arugula, oakleaf, frisée
4 to 6 ripe red tomatoes, quartered

1. Wash and dry the chickens and set them aside.

2. In the work bowl of a food processor, combine the cheese, scallions, 4 tablespoons of the olive oil, vinegar, garlic, basil, and salt and pepper to taste. Pulse to blend roughly; do not over-process to make a smooth mixture.

3. Stuff the chickens under the skin with the cheese mixture. Gently lift the skin away from the chickens at the neck end and from the bottom, and push the mixture under, using your fingers. Take care not to tear the skin. Press gently on the skin to spread and evenly distribute the stuffing.

4. Whisk together the remaining 2 tablespoons olive oil and the lemon juice and brush the mixture over the chickens on both sides. Place the chickens in a porcelain or glass dish, cover with plastic wrap, and refrigerate for 2 or more hours.

5. Remove the chickens from the refrigerator 15 minutes before cooking. Prepare a charcoal fire or heat the broiler (charcoal is far superior for this dish). When the fire is ready, cook the chickens on both sides, bone side first, brushing with any remaining lemon-oil mixture. If you are using a kettle-type grill, you may want to cover it for part of the cooking time. The chicken should be deep golden brown but not charred, which would compromise the flavor of the stuffing. Set aside.

6. Place the dressing ingredients in the work bowl of a food processor and process until the mixture is smooth. Toss the lettuces with the vinaigrette in a large salad bowl. Place the lettuces on a very large platter and arrange the chickens on top; arrange the tomatoes alongside the chickens. Or, arrange the salad and chickens on individual plates, and garnish with the tomatoes.

☞ **NOTE**: The lettuces can be cleaned hours ahead of time, and the dressing made and stored in a covered jar. The chicken however, will not be as successful if grilled and then kept refrigerated.

Fresh ricotta cheese, drained of excess liquid, can be substituted for the goat cheese, in which case you will have New Italian Chicken Salad.

MICHAEL'S GRILLED CHICKEN AND GOAT CHEESE SALAD

This salad, which is featured at Michael McCarty's namesake restaurants in New York and Santa Monica, almost single-handedly defines the California-American cooking style. Its conspicuous elements include grilling, baby lettuces, salsa, and, by no means least of all, domestic goat cheese. Those may have been some of the hallmarks of the most creative American chefs of the seventies and eighties but they are now part of the repertoire of millions of home cooks. I simplified the recipe slightly, incorporating McCarty's tomato concasse into the vinaigrette.

✗ *6 servings*

6 chicken breast halves, boned, skin on, and wing bones attached

One 12-ounce log fresh California goat cheese, cut into ¼-inch slices

Salt

Freshly ground black pepper

3 red bell peppers, stems and seeds removed, cut into 1-inch-wide strips

3 yellow bell peppers, stems and seeds removed, cut into 1-inch-wide strips

1 large or 2 small sweet onions, such as Maui, Vidalia, Walla Walla, or red, peeled and cut into ⅜-inch slices

2 tablespoons extra-virgin olive oil

1 bunch chives, snipped

DRESSING

1⅓ cups extra-virgin olive oil

⅔ cup balsamic vinegar

Juice of 1 lime

½ small shallot, peeled and minced

1 tablespoon finely chopped basil leaves

2 medium ripe tomatoes, peeled, seeded, and cubed

SALSA

2 jalapeño peppers, peeled seeded and minced

2 tablespoons chopped fresh cilantro leaves

1 cup extra-virgin olive oil

Juice of 2 limes

• • • • • • • • •

3 heads limestone lettuce, washed, dried, and torn

3 bunches mâche, washed and dried (about 2 cups)

2 bunches arugula, washed, dried, and torn

1 small head radicchio, leaves torn

1. Prepare a charcoal fire or preheat the broiler.

2. Using your finger, gently lift the skin on the long side of the breasts and insert the goat cheese slices, overlapping them slightly and leaving the skin attached on the opposite side. Season the breasts to taste with salt and freshly ground pepper.

3. Brush the pepper strips and onion slices lightly with the olive oil and set them aside.

4. When the fire is ready, grill the chicken, skin side up, for 3 to 5 minutes, then turn and grill for 5 to 7 minutes on the skin side. Remove the chicken to a platter.

5. Grill the pepper strips and onion slices for about 30 seconds per side, to lightly char and heat through.

6. Whisk together the dressing ingredients, except for the tomatoes; season to taste with salt and pepper and stir in the tomatoes.

7. Whisk together the ingredients for the salsa.

8. Toss the greens together in a large bowl, then divide them among 6 individual plates. Cut each chicken breast into 4 or 5 slices and place them alongside the greens. Place the grilled vegetables on the greens. Dress the greens and vegetables with the dressing; spoon the salsa over the chicken. Sprinkle the chives over all.

☛**NOTE:** Other greens can be substituted, but try to find young, tender ones and a good combination. The dressing and salsa can be made in advance and refrigerated until needed, but the lime juice should not be added to the salsa until the last moment or it will discolor the cilantro.

NEW YEAR'S EVE CHICKEN SALAD

This is simple but elegant, and suitable for any festive occasion, as a first course or light midnight supper. ✗ *6 servings*

6 medium new potatoes

3 whole poached chicken breasts, separated, skinned, boned, and shredded

2 heads Boston lettuce, separated into leaves, washed, and dried

DRESSING

½ cup neutral-flavored oil, such as soy or safflower

2 teaspoons freshly squeezed lemon juice

2 tablespoons minced Italian parsley

2 tablespoons snipped chives

•   •   •   •   •   •   •   •   •   •

½ pint commercial crème fraîche

1 ounce fresh caviar

Additional snipped chives

1. Bring a medium-large pot of water to a boil. Wash but do not peel the potatoes. Drop them in the water and boil until they are just cooked through; do not overcook. Refresh the potatoes immediately under cold water and peel them. When the potatoes are cool enough to handle, cut them into matchsticks and place them in a mixing bowl with the chicken.

2. Whisk together the ingredients for the dressing and pour it over the chicken and potatoes. Toss to combine very gently so that the potato sticks do not break up.

3. Using one or more leaves as necessary to make cups, place the lettuce leaves on 6 individual plates. Divide the chicken-potato mixture among the cups. Place a generous dollop of crème fraîche and a spoonful of caviar on each mound of chicken. Garnish with additional chives.

☞ **NOTE**: I always use Sevruga caviar because it is my favorite. Use your favorite, and of course, you can increase the amount according to the occasion, the company, and your pocketbook.

CURRIED CHICKEN SALAD

✗ *6 to 8 servings*

½ cup golden raisins
½ cup apple juice
3 whole poached chicken breasts, cubed
3 to 4 stalks celery, trimmed, washed, and cut into ½-inch slices (about 1 cup)
1 medium green apple, washed, unpeeled, and cubed

DRESSING
1 cup low- or nonfat plain yogurt
1 teaspoon curry powder

1 teaspoon ground cumin
2 teaspoons white wine vinegar
¼ cup fruit from commercial mango chutney, minced
Tabasco or similar hot pepper sauce
• • • • • • • • • •
½ cup chopped cilantro or parsley leaves
1 cup whole toasted almonds, roughly chopped

1. Place the raisins in a small bowl. Warm the apple juice and add to the bowl; let the raisins plump for 5 to 10 minutes. Drain, reserving the liquid.

2. Combine the chicken, raisins, celery, and apple in a serving dish.

3. Whisk together the ingredients for the dressing, adding dashes of the Tabasco sauce to taste. Taste the dressing carefully; there should be a good balance of hot, sweet, and tangy flavors. Pour the dressing onto the salad ingredients and toss carefully to combine. Sprinkle the cilantro and chopped almonds over and serve.

COBB SALAD

By the time I moved to Los Angeles, in the 1970s, the Brown Derby's moment as one of Hollywood's smartest hangouts had long passed, and only a rube from back east would give a second glance to a restaurant built to resemble a hat. The Derby's signature dish persists, however, and interpretations abound, some from cooks completely ignorant of its provenance. In this version, the avocado, which is an essential element, is echoed in the tangy dressing, and of course chicken replaces the traditional turkey.

✖ *6 servings*

2 heads romaine lettuce

Meat from one 3- to 3½-pound grilled or broiled chicken, from 2 whole poached breasts, or from 1 small (3 to 3½ pounds) or ½ large (6 to 7 pounds) roasted chicken, cut into strips

6 slices bacon, cooked crisp, drained, and crumbled

1 large or 2 small avocados, peeled and pitted, the flesh cut into long thin slices

½ cup Roquefort or other blue-veined cheese, crumbled

2 ripe tomatoes, cut into wedges

DRESSING

1 large or 2 small avocados, peeled, pitted, and cut into chunks

2 tablespoons freshly squeezed lemon juice

2 tablespoons olive oil

⅓ cup low- or nonfat plain yogurt

Salt

Freshly ground black pepper

1. Discard any tough, torn, or discolored outer leaves from the lettuce. Tear the remaining leaves into medium-sized pieces from the larger ribs; the smallest tender inner leaves can be left intact.

2. Divide the lettuce among 6 rimmed dinner plates or shallow soup plates. Arrange the chicken, bacon, avocados, and cheese in rows over the lettuce. Place the tomatoes around the edges of the plates.

3. Place the avocado chunks, lemon juice, olive oil, and yogurt in the work bowl of a food processor; process to blend to a smooth purée. Season to taste with salt and pepper; taste and adjust with additional lemon juice if necessary or with additional yogurt if needed to achieve the texture of thick cream.

4. Drizzle a bit of dressing across each salad and pass the additional dressing at the table.

CHICKEN SALAD "CEVICHE"

*C*hicken can't be "cooked" in citrus juices the way seafood can, but it has a delicate nature that similarly lends itself to the vibrant, refreshing flavors of a typical ceviche. This works best as an appetizer, particularly to precede grilled foods on a warm evening. ✕ *6 servings as appetizer, 4 servings as entrée*

4 whole poached chicken breasts, skinned and separated

1 large red or yellow pepper, trimmed of stem and seeds

2 ripe avocados

Tender inside leaves of 1 or 2 heads romaine lettuce

MARINADE

Juice of 6 or 7 limes (about ¾ cup)

¼ cup olive oil

½ red onion, peeled and chopped

1 jalapeño or similar hot pepper, minced

1. Cut the breasts lengthwise into thin pieces not more than ½ inch thick. Place the chicken in 1 layer in a shallow glass or porcelain dish.

2. Whisk together the marinade and pour it over the chicken. Turn the chicken to coat it completely. Cover the dish with plastic wrap and refrigerate for 2 to 4 hours.

3. Cut the pepper lengthwise into very thin slices. Peel the avocados and cut them lengthwise into thin slices. Arrange the lettuce leaves on a serving platter or individual plates.

4. Using a slotted spoon, lift the chicken out of the marinade, letting the excess fall back into the dish. Arrange the chicken over the lettuce. Arrange the pepper and avocado slices over and alongside the chicken. Drizzle some of the marinade over the vegetables to moisten them a bit.

PORTUGUESE CHICKEN SALAD

✗ *6 servings*

3 cups cut-up grilled, broiled,
   or roasted chicken
1 tablespoon drained capers
12 large basil leaves, chopped
3 tablespoons diced pimientos
12 medium green olives, the flesh
   cut off the stones in pieces
½ cup roughly chopped Italian
   parsley leaves
4 to 6 anchovies, drained and
   chopped
¼ to ½ cup olive oil
6 slices sturdy peasant or country
   bread

DRESSING
1 large ripe tomato, peeled,
   seeded, and roughly chopped
6 to 8 tablespoons virgin olive oil
2 teaspoons red wine vinegar
Salt
Freshly ground black pepper

• • • • • • • • • •

3 tomatoes, cut into 6 wedges each
12 or so black oil-cured olives

1. Combine the chicken, capers, basil, pimientos, green olives, parsley, and anchovies in a serving dish.

2. Heat a heavy skillet over medium-high heat. Add enough oil to just cover the bottom of the skillet; add the bread slices and brown quickly on both sides, adding oil as needed. Drain the bread on paper towels and set aside.

3. Place the dressing ingredients in the work bowl of a food processor and process to blend well, starting with 6 tablespoons olive oil and adding 1 or 2 tablespoons more to achieve a smooth texture and balanced flavor. Season with salt and freshly ground black pepper.

4. Pour the dressing over the salad ingredients and toss to combine well. Cut the bread slices in half and place around the dish. Garnish with the black olives. Alternatively, divide the salad among 6 plates, place the bread on either side, and garnish each portion with the tomatoes and black olives.

CHICKEN TONNATO

C hicken makes perfect sense as a substitute for veal in this classic Italian cold dish. The delicacy of the poached chicken offers the same foil to the rich, emphatically flavored dressing.
✕ 6 servings

3 whole poached chicken breasts, boned, skinned, and separated
2 to 3 heads Bibb lettuce, trimmed, washed, and dried
½ cup coarsely chopped Italian parsley
2 lemons, thinly sliced
3 tablespoons drained capers
18 oil-cured black olives
3 hard-boiled eggs, coarsely chopped (optional)

DRESSING

½ cup extra-virgin olive oil
1 egg yolk, at room temperature
One 6-ounce can Italian tuna fish, packed in oil if possible, well drained
4 anchovy fillets, well drained and cut up
¼ cup freshly squeezed lemon juice
¼ cup cold heavy cream

1. Using a sharp knife, diagonally cut each breast into 4 or 5 medium-thick slices.

2. To make the dressing, combine the oil, egg yolk, tuna, anchovies, and lemon juice in the work bowl of a food processor and process just to blend well; it is not necessary to make a perfectly smooth purée.

3. Scrape the purée into a bowl and stir in the cream.

4. Arrange the lettuce leaves on a serving platter, and arrange the chicken slices down the center, overlapping slightly. Spoon the dressing over the chicken slices, masking them almost, but not quite, completely. Sprinkle the parsley over the sauce and arrange the lemon slices, capers, and olives along the sides, and the eggs at the ends of the platter. Pass any remaining dressing at the table.

☛ **NOTE**: Alternatively, the chicken can be cut into chunks and tossed with the dressing, then garnished with the remaining ingredients.

ZARELA'S ENSALADA GIRASOL

*Z*arela Martinez is the proprietor of Zarela, one of New York's *few fine Mexican restaurants. Zarela's cuisine is at once authentic and highly personal. This, with slight adjustment, is a dish that reflects both aspects of the restaurant's style. It is also one of its most popular. ✕6 servings*

3 whole chicken breasts, boned but with the skin on; separated

2 large ripe mangoes, peeled, seeded, and thinly sliced

1 large jicama, peeled and cut into fine julienne or diced

MARINADE

One 8-ounce can chiles chipotles en adobo

4 or 5 garlic cloves, peeled and roughly chopped

1 tablespoon dried oregano, preferably Mexican

3 tablespoons olive or vegetable oil

DRESSING

2 or 3 chiles chipotles en adobo, minced

1 garlic clove, peeled and minced

1 teaspoon dried oregano, preferably Mexican

½ cup red wine vinegar

1 cup olive oil

1. Place the chicken breasts in 1 layer in a glass or porcelain dish. Place the chiles for the marinade in the work bowl of a food processor and purée. Add the remaining marinade ingredients and pulse or turn the machine on and off to incorporate, but leave somewhat textured. Brush the marinade over the chicken and set aside at cool room temperature or in the refrigerator for 30 minutes or so. Start a charcoal fire or heat the broiler. Cook the chicken for 4 to 6 minutes per side, until browned and crisped and cooked through. Set aside for about 15 minutes.

2. Whisk together the ingredients for the dressing. Pour about ⅓ of the dressing over the mangoes, and another third over the jicama. Using a slotted spoon or spatula, lift the mangoes from the dressing and arrange, sunflower-fashion, around 6 individual plates. Lift the jicama from its dressing and arrange in the center of each plate.

3. Slice the chicken on the diagonal and toss with the remaining dressing (use the dressing left from the mangoes and jicama if it is needed). Pile the chicken on top of the jicama and serve.

PACIFIC NORTHWEST CHICKEN SALAD

✻ *6 servings*

Salt

1 pound Yukon gold or yellow Finn potatoes, smallest possible

1 large Walla Walla or other sweet onion, peeled

3 cups cubed grilled, broiled, roasted, or poached chicken

4 hard-boiled, eggs, peeled and roughly chopped

½ cup sliced celery

2 tablespoons snipped chives

DRESSING

1 scant cup mayonnaise

¼ cup Dijon mustard

2 tablespoons white wine vinegar

¼ to ½ teaspoon cracked black pepper

1. Bring a large pot of water to a boil; add a pinch of salt and the potatoes. Boil until the potatoes are just tender. Drain, refresh under cold water, and drain well; set aside.

2. Cut the onion in half lengthwise and then slice thinly crosswise. Place the onion, chicken, eggs, and celery in a serving dish. When the potatoes are cool enough to handle, cut them into halves or quarters, depending on their size (the pieces should relate in size to the other ingredients); do not peel the potatoes.

3. Whisk together the ingredients for the dressing and pour it into the bowl; toss gently to combine. Sprinkle the chives over the salad and serve.

KEN HOM'S
EAST MEETS WEST
CHICKEN SALAD

K*en Hom, a Chinese American who lives in Berkeley, California, and teaches cooking classes in Hong Kong is the natural practitioner of the East-West cooking style. That style is exemplified in this dish. East-West does not refer only to the movement of Asian ingredients into Western cooking; the movement can be in either direction. Hom points out that European asparagus is still relatively rare in Asia, but has become popular in cosmopolitan Hong Kong. The dressing, on the other hand, is basically French, with a slight Eastern accent. ✕ 6 servings as appetizer, 4 servings as entrée*

½ pound asparagus, cut diagonally into 2-inch slices

2 whole chicken breasts, boned, skinned, and separated; cut into 3-inch by ¼-inch strips

3 tablespoons shredded sun-dried tomatoes

1 cup loosely packed basil leaves

3 tablespoons finely chopped scallions

2 commercial pickled red sweet peppers, drained and cut into strips

DRESSING

1 egg yolk

1 teaspoon Dijon mustard

Salt

Freshly ground black pepper

2 teaspoons minced garlic

2 teaspoons Chinese sesame paste

¼ cup peanut oil

¼ cup olive oil

1. Bring a medium-sized pot of water to a boil; drop the asparagus in briefly—about 30 seconds—and remove with a slotted spoon. Refresh the asparagus immediately under cold water and drain.

2. Add the chicken to the water; turn off the heat, cover the pot, and steep the chicken for 4 minutes. Drain the chicken and refresh it under cold water.

3. For the dressing, beat together the egg yolk, mustard, and salt and pepper to taste. Add the garlic and sesame paste and mix well. Add the oils in a slow steady stream, beating continuously as if making mayonnaise, until the oil is fully incorporated.

4. In a serving dish, toss the chicken and asparagus with the dressing. Add the sun-dried tomatoes, basil leaves, and scallions and toss again. Top with the peppers and serve.

☛ **NOTE**: The egg yolk can be omitted from the dressing.

WOLFGANG PUCK'S MINCED GARLIC CHICKEN

Puck's celebrity as one of the country's leading chefs is deserved: His several visually stunning restaurants are showcases for creative, eclectic menus, and his kitchens operate at a consistently high level. This dish is served at Chinois in Santa Monica, California, and is Wolf's interpretation of the minced squab that is featured in some Chinese restaurants. Chicken carries the concept well, and radicchio brings color and more flavor than the usual iceberg lettuce.

✂ 4 servings

¾ pound ground raw chicken meat, white, dark, or mixed

3 scallions, trimmed and minced

Salt

Freshly ground black pepper

DRESSING

2 tablespoons rice wine vinegar

1 tablespoon soy sauce

1 tablespoon peanut oil

1 tablespoon sesame oil

1 tablespoon sherry wine vinegar

• • • • • • • • • •

1 cup densely packed watercress leaves

½ cup julienned celery

½ cup julienned carrots

½ cup julienned onion

2 tablespoons peanut oil

1½ tablespoons finely chopped garlic

1 tablespoon finely chopped ginger

¼ teaspoon red pepper flakes

¼ cup rice wine vinegar

¼ cup plum wine

2 tablespoons soy sauce

¼ cup chicken broth

8 to 12 whole radicchio leaves, depending on size

2 tablespoons chopped fresh cilantro or mint

1. In a small bowl, combine the chicken and scallions and season lightly with salt and pepper; set aside.

2. In a medium bowl, whisk together the ingredients for the dressing. Add the watercress, celery, carrots, and onion and toss to combine; season with salt and pepper to taste.

3. Heat the peanut oil in a large skillet until it is smoking. Form the chicken into one large patty and carefully set it in the pan. Brown on one side, then stir in the garlic, ginger, and red pepper flakes. Break up the patty and continue to stir until the chicken is completely browned. Pour in the rice wine vinegar, plum wine, soy sauce, and broth and continue to cook until most of the liquid has evaporated.

4. Use the radicchio leaves to form 4 cups and set them on individual plates. Divide first the watercress salad, then the chicken mixture among the radicchio cups, and top with the cilantro or mint. Encourage your guests to roll the leaves and salad up like tacos and to eat them with their hands.

COLD SOMEN NOODLES
WITH CHICKEN

*C*hicken salad as such doesn't exist in Japanese cooking, but numerous cold dishes do, some of which involve noodles in combination with other ingredients and delicate sauces. Chicken, in this case marinated with typical ingredients and then grilled, is highly compatible with somen noodles, which frequently form the basis of cold noodle dishes. ✕6 servings

3 whole chicken breasts, skinned, boned, and separated

Salt

¼ pound somen noodles (*tomoshi-raga*)

½ pound asparagus, as thin as possible

1 cucumber, peeled

MARINADE

½ cup soy sauce

¼ cup rice wine vinegar

1 garlic clove, peeled and minced

1 teaspoon light sesame, soy, or peanut oil

2 teaspoons sugar

DRESSING

1 tablespoon wasabi powder

½ cup rice wine vinegar

2 tablespoons soy sauce

1 teaspoon sugar

1 teaspoon light sesame, soy, or peanut oil

• • • • • • • • • •

2 bunches salad spinach or watercress, trimmed and washed (optional)

3 or 4 scallions, trimmed, with 2 inches green tops retained

1. Place the chicken breasts in a glass or porcelain dish that will hold them in 1 layer. Whisk together the ingredients for the marinade and pour over the chicken; turn the breasts to coat them evenly. Cover the dish with plastic wrap and refrigerate for 4 hours or up to overnight.

2. Take the chicken out of the refrigerator about 15 minutes before cooking. Prepare a charcoal fire or heat the broiler. Cook the chicken for 4 or 5 minutes per side, until nicely browned and crisped on the outside and cooked through. Set aside.

3. Meanwhile, bring a pot of water to a boil. Add a pinch of salt and the noodles. Cook the noodles al dente, which will take only 2 to 3 minutes; take care not to overcook them. Drain and refresh immediately under cold water; set the noodles aside.

4. Snap off the ends of the asparagus. If they are very, very thin, like the grassy asparagus sometimes available in early spring, leave them as they are. If they are thicker, cut off the tips and cut them lengthwise into 2 or 3 thin strands. Bring a pot of water to a boil. Add a pinch of salt and the asparagus and cook briefly, about a minute; the asparagus should be quite crunchy. Drain, refresh immediately under cold water, drain again, and set aside.

5. Cut the cucumber in half lengthwise and remove the seeds. Cut the cucumber in half crosswise if it is very long, then in half lengthwise and into very thin strands. Add the cucumber to the asparagus.

6. Combine the noodles, asparagus, and cucumber in a mixing bowl. Mix the wasabi in a mixing bowl with enough water— about 1 tablespoon—to make a paste. Add the rest of the dressing ingredients and pour over the noodles and vegetables.

7. Cut the chicken diagonally into thin slices. Place the spinach leaves or watercress on a serving platter or individual plates and mound the noodle mixture in the center. Arrange the chicken on top, and drizzle over any juices that have accumulated from it. Cut the scallions into thin diagonal slices and sprinkle over all.

☛ **NOTE:** Cutting the asparagus into strands may seem bothersome, but it is not difficult or time-consuming for such a small amount. It is worth the effort for the nice presentation it makes. Nevertheless, the asparagus may be cut into 2-inch diagonal pieces if you like.

Chicken Salads with Vegetables

BROCCOLI AND PASTA CHICKEN SALAD

✕ *6 generous servings*

Salt

½ pound short tubular pasta such as penne or cut ziti, preferably whole wheat

4 stalks fresh broccoli

Meat from one 3½-pound broiled chicken cubed

2 tablespoons olive oil

2 garlic cloves, peeled and chopped

3 or 4 anchovies packed in oil, drained and cut into 3 or 4 pieces each

⅓ cup mayonnaise

½ cup chopped parsley

2 teaspoons freshly squeezed lemon juice

1. Bring a large pot of water to a boil; add salt and the pasta.

2. Trim the broccoli. Separate the florets from the stalks. Peel the stalks and cut them into pieces about ¼ inch wide by about 2½ inches long. When the pasta is within 2 minutes of being al dente, add the broccoli. Cook for about 2 minutes; the pasta should be al dente and the broccoli still a bit crisp. Drain and refresh well under cold water. Drain again and turn into a large serving dish. Add the chicken to the dish.

3. Warm the oil in a small heavy skillet; add the garlic and cook until golden brown. Add the anchovies and cook briefly; they should break down and soften. Pour the contents of the pan into a small bowl. Cool for a few minutes.

4. Add the mayonnaise, parsley, and lemon juice to the bowl containing the anchovies and whisk to blend well. Add the dressing to the serving dish and toss to combine before serving.

CHICKEN SALAD
RÉMOULADE

n Mastering the Art of French Cooking *Julia Child lets us know in no uncertain terms that celery rémoulade does not imply sauce rémoulade, another thing altogether. This, therefore, must be considered a dish derived from both those icons of the French repertoire.* ✖*8 to 10 servings as appetizer, 6 servings as entrée*

One 1-pound celery root
2 teaspoons lemon juice
2 teaspoons coarse salt
3 whole chicken breasts, poached

DRESSING
4 or 5 cornichon or similar small
  pickles, drained and minced
¼ cup drained capers
3 or 4 anchovies in oil, drained
  and minced
1 scant cup mayonnaise

1 tablespoon Dijon mustard
1 tablespoon freshly squeezed
  lemon juice
¼ cup finely chopped parsley,
  chives, and tarragon, mixed
Freshly ground white pepper

• • • • • • • • • •

2 cups shredded soft lettuce leaves
  such as Boston or Bibb
2 hard-boiled eggs, roughly
  chopped

1. Carefully trim and peel the celery root and cut it into matchstick-thin julienne. Combine the celery root with the lemon juice and coarse salt and set aside for about 30 minutes. Rinse and drain well the celery root; set aside.

2. Cut or tear the chicken breasts into long thin juliennelike pieces. Place the celery root and chicken in a mixing bowl.

3. Whisk together the ingredients for the dressing and toss it with the chicken and celery root. Arrange the lettuce on a platter or individual plates and mound the salad in the center. Garnish with the chopped eggs.

BEET-CHICKEN SALAD

❌6 servings

Salt

5 medium beets, washed and
trimmed

1 medium cucumber

5 scallions, trimmed, with 2 inches
green tops retained

6 radishes, washed and trimmed

5 cups cubed poached or roasted
chicken

DRESSING

½ cup low- or nonfat plain yogurt

½ cup buttermilk

2 tablespoons lemon juice

1 tablespoon Dijon mustard

⅓ cup snipped dill

Salt

Freshly ground pepper

I. Bring a medium-sized pot of water to a boil; add a pinch
of salt and the beets. Cook at a low boil until the beets are just tender when pierced with a knife; take care not to overcook them.
Drain and refresh immediately under cold water. When the beets
are cool enough to handle, peel them and cut them into quarters,
and then cut each piece in half. Set aside.

2. Peel the cucumber only if it is waxed. Cut it in half lengthwise, remove the seeds, and cut crosswise into ½-inch slices.

3. Slice the scallions and the radishes.

4. Whisk together the ingredients for the dressing; taste and
adjust the seasonings as necessary. Season with salt and freshly
ground pepper to taste.

5. Combine the beets, cucumber, scallions, radishes, and
chicken in a serving dish with the dressing. Toss to combine, and
serve.

☞**NOTE:** Although the components can be prepared in
advance, they should not be combined until just before serving or
the salad will become pink and watery.

CHICKEN AND GREENS SALAD

The inspiration for this comes from the Southern tradition of serving fried chicken with greens, but here the greens are fresh and crisp, rather than "cooked down." The chicken coating is typical of that used for frying catfish; this good idea comes from Michael McLaughlin's **The New American Kitchen.** ✖6 servings

3 whole chicken breasts, separated, skinned, boned, and lightly pounded (6 chicken cutlets)
1 cup buttermilk
½ cup all-purpose flour
½ cup yellow cornmeal
1 teaspoon dried thyme
1 teaspoon paprika
Salt
Freshly ground pepper
¼ cup (about) peanut or corn oil

DRESSING
1 tablespoon Dijon mustard
2 tablespoons white wine vinegar
1 teaspoon hot pepper vinegar, or hot pepper sauce such as Tabasco
½ cup peanut oil
¼ cup olive oil

• • • • • • • • • •

8 cups fresh young dandelion greens, washed and dried
1 medium red onion, peeled and sliced into thin rings

1. Place the chicken in a bowl and cover it with the buttermilk. Leave at cool room temperature or in the refrigerator for 2 hours or longer.

2. On a sheet of wax paper, combine the flour, cornmeal, thyme, paprika, and salt and pepper to taste.

3. Remove the pieces of chicken from the buttermilk, letting most of it drip off. Coat the pieces in the cornmeal mixture and place them on a platter or another sheet of wax paper for 30 minutes.

4. Heat a large heavy skillet (cast-iron is best) and pour in enough oil to cover the bottom generously. Cook the chicken in the oil until it is golden brown and crisp, 3 to 4 minutes per side. Set the chicken on paper towels.

5. Whisk together the ingredients for the dressing in a large bowl. Taste and adjust with salt and pepper and additional hot pepper vinegar to taste—the dressing should have some zing. Add the dandelion greens to the bowl and toss well.

6. Place the greens on a large platter and scatter the onion rings over. Cut each piece of chicken into 3 or 4 diagonal slices and place over the onion.

☛**NOTE**: Other greens, such as young collards, turnips, beets, or escarole, can be substituted for the dandelions or used in combination.

CHICKEN SALAD PUNJAB

✕ 6 servings

MARINADE

½ cup low- or nonfat plain yogurt

3 garlic cloves, peeled

1 jalapeño pepper, cut in half, and trimmed of stem and seeds

1 teaspoon whole cumin seeds

1 teaspoon ground cumin

½ teaspoon ground cayenne

Generous dash cinnamon

• • • • • • • •

3 whole boned and skinned chicken breasts, separated

1 medium head cauliflower

Salt

⅓ cup currants

½ cup chicken broth

¼ cup roughly chopped cilantro leaves or Italian parsley leaves

⅓ cup whole almonds, toasted and roughly chopped

DRESSING

¾ cup low- or nonfat plain yogurt

1 teaspoon curry powder

¼ teaspoon ground cumin

1 teaspoon white wine vinegar

1. Place the marinade ingredients in the work bowl of a food processor and pulse or turn on and off to make a rough-textured mixture; the mixture will be thick, almost pasty. Coat the chicken breasts on both sides with the marinade and place them in a glass or porcelain dish; cover with plastic wrap and refrigerate for at least 6 hours or overnight. Remove the chicken from the refrigerator about 15 minutes before you wish to cook it.

2. Trim the cauliflower and cut into florets; cut them in half if they seem large. Bring a large pot of water to a boil, add a large pinch of salt, and add the cauliflower. Cook for about 5 minutes, or until the cauliflower is just tender; do not overcook. Drain the cauliflower, refresh immediately under cold water, drain again, and set aside.

3. Place the currants in a small bowl. Warm the broth and pour it over the currants; plump the currants for about 5 minutes, then drain, reserving the liquid.

4. Prepare a charcoal fire or heat a broiler. When the fire is ready, cook the chicken for 4 to 5 minutes on each side, until crisp and brown on the outside and cooked through. Set the chicken aside for 15 minutes.

5. Whisk together the dressing ingredients, along with the reserved currant-plumping liquid.

6. Cut the chicken on the bias into thick slices. Combine the chicken in a serving dish with the cauliflower and the currants, and toss with the dressing. Sprinkle with the cilantro or parsley and the almonds and serve.

SPRING CHICKEN SALAD

✕6 servings

Salt
½ pound orzo or riso (rice-shaped pasta)
1 pound fresh asparagus
1 cup shelled fresh young peas
¼ cup buttermilk
½ cup sour cream
⅓ cup snipped chives
Freshly ground white or black pepper

3 cups cubed poached or roasted chicken
2 tablespoons chervil leaves, or roughly chopped Italian parsley leaves
3 scallions, trimmed, with 1 inch green tops retained and thinly sliced

1. Bring a medium-sized pot of water to a boil; add a pinch of salt and the pasta. Cook the pasta until just al dente; drain, refresh under cold water, and drain again well.

2. Trim the ends off the asparagus and cut off the tips. Set the tips aside and cut the stalks into 3 or 4 pieces. Bring a medium-sized pot of water to a boil; add a pinch of salt and the asparagus stalks. Cook the stalks for 1 to 3 minutes, depending on their thickness, until just barely tender; drop in the tips and cook for 1 minute longer. Drain the asparagus and refresh immediately under cold water; drain well. Pick out the tips and set them aside.

3. If the peas are very young, small, and tender, they do not need to be cooked. If they are not, steam them for 1 to 2 minutes in a small pan or in a microwave oven. Add the peas to the asparagus tips.

4. Place the cooked asparagus stalks, buttermilk, and sour cream in the work bowl of a food processor and process to blend well. The mixture should have the consistency of thick cream; add additional teaspoons of buttermilk if necessary. Add the chives to the mixture and season with salt and freshly ground white or black pepper.

5. Combine the pasta, asparagus tips, peas, and chicken in a serving bowl. Add the dressing and toss to combine well. Sprinkle with the chervil or parsley and the scallions and serve.

POTATO AND CHICKEN SALAD

✕ *4 to 6 servings*

1 pound small new potatoes
Salt
¼ pound pancetta, diced
2 packed cups large basil leaves
3 cups cubed grilled, broiled, or
  roasted chicken

DRESSING
1 head Roasted Garlic (page 29)
¾ cup mayonnaise
1 teaspoon red wine vinegar
Pinch crushed hot red pepper
  flakes

1. Scrub the potatoes but do not peel them. Bring a large pot of water to a boil; add a pinch of salt and the potatoes. Cook the potatoes until they are just tender when pierced with a sharp knife; do not overcook them. Drain them and refresh them under cold water; drain well and set aside.

2. Place the pancetta in a small heavy skillet over medium-high heat and cook, turning, until crisp and browned. Remove the pancetta with a slotted spoon and drain on paper towels.

3. Stack the basil leaves and cut them crosswise into ½-inch pieces.

4. Place the garlic cloves, mayonnaise, vinegar, and pepper flakes in the work bowl of a food processor and process till creamy.

5. If the potatoes are very small—an inch or so in diameter—do not cut them. If they are larger, cut them into halves or quarters. Place the potatoes, pancetta, and chicken in a serving dish. Toss gently to combine. Pour the dressing over and toss again. Sprinkle the basil over and serve.

ARTICHOKE CHICKEN SALAD

This "salad" defines the idea of a one-dish meal; it is hearty, substantial, and full of flavor. ✕ 6 to 8 servings

1 large (6 to 7 pounds) chicken,
   roasted, pan juices reserved
3 large artichokes
1 lemon
Salt
¾ pound shiitake, cremini, or other
   mushrooms
1 tablespoon olive oil
¼ cup chicken stock
2 tablespoons coarsely chopped
   Italian parsley
¼ pound Gruyère cheese, diced

DRESSING
1 head Roasted Garlic (page 29)
Pan drippings from chicken,
   completely defatted
2 teaspoons fresh thyme leaves
¼ to ⅓ cup chicken stock
Salt
Freshly ground white or black
   pepper

1. Pour the reserved chicken-cooking juices into a small bowl and place in the refrigerator or freezer. When the fat has risen to the surface and is somewhat solidified, carefully remove and discard it; you should have ¼ cup or so of rich, fat-free drippings.

2. Squeeze the juice from the lemon into a large bowl of water.

3. To prepare the artichokes, trim the stem off each at the base. Cut or break away all the tough, dark outer leaves until you reach the pale green-white inner part. Using a large kitchen knife, cut the tops off about 1½ inches above the base; trim the bases. Cut the artichokes into quarters. Using the tip of a paring knife, carefully remove the hairy choke from the center of each wedge, then cut each wedge into 3 pieces. Trim the ends from the stems, peel them, and cut them lengthwise into pieces of roughly the same thickness as the slices from the heart. As you work, drop the artichoke pieces into the water.

4. Bring a large pot of water to a boil, add a generous pinch of salt, and drop in the artichokes. Cook just until tender when pierced with a knife, 3 to 5 minutes; take care not to overcook the artichokes or they will become mushy and tasteless. Drain them and refresh immediately under cold water. Drain again and set aside.

5. Trim the stems from the mushrooms and cut the caps into slices about ¼ inch wide. Warm the oil in a medium-sized skillet over medium-high heat. Add the mushrooms and toss briefly; add the stock and continue to cook until the mushrooms are lightly colored, 1 to 2 minutes (most of the liquid will have been absorbed). Remove the mushrooms from the heat, add the parsley, and set aside.

6. Remove the meat from the chicken and cut or tear it into large pieces. Combine the chicken, artichokes, and mushrooms in a large shallow serving dish.

7. Place the cloves of roasted garlic and the pan juices in the work bowl of a food processor and process to blend well. Add the thyme leaves. Pour the stock through the feed tube while the machine is running until the dressing is the consistency of thick cream. Season to taste with salt and freshly ground white or black pepper. Pour the dressing over the chicken mixture and toss to coat evenly. Toss the Gruyère over everything and serve.

CHICKEN SALAD SICILIANA

✂ *6 to 8 servings*

3 whole chicken breasts, skinned
and boned

MARINADE
½ cup orange juice
1 tablespoon virgin olive oil
1 large garlic clove, peeled and
minced
1 tablespoon dry marsala wine
• • • • • • • • • •
1 medium fennel bulb
½ medium red onion
3 blood oranges, or 2 navel oranges

DRESSING
½ cup virgin olive oil
3 tablespoons orange juice
2 tablespoons dry marsala wine
1 teaspoon cracked pepper
Pinch salt
• • • • • • • • • •
2 heads romaine lettuce, tender
inner leaves only
½ cup fresh mint leaves

I. Place the chicken breasts in 1 layer in a glass or porcelain dish. Whisk together the ingredients for the marinade and pour over the breasts; turn the breasts over, cover with plastic wrap, and refrigerate for at least 6 hours or overnight.

2. Prepare a charcoal fire or heat the broiler. Cook the breasts for 4 to 5 minutes on each side, basting with any remaining marinade. Let the chicken rest for 15 minutes.

3. Trim the fennel bulb at the root end and at the top of the bulb. Cut the bulb in half from top to bottom; cut away the core and cut each half crosswise into thin slices. Place the fennel in a large mixing bowl.

4. Peel the onion and cut it in half top to bottom; cut each half crosswise into thin slices. Add the onion to the bowl with the fennel.

5. Peel the oranges, carefully removing the pith from the flesh; separate each section, cutting away the membranes. Add the orange sections to the bowl.

6. Cut the chicken diagonally into ½-inch pieces and add to the bowl.

7. Whisk together the dressing ingredients; taste for seasoning and adjust. Pour the dressing over the other ingredients and toss carefully.

8. Arrange the romaine lettuce leaves on a large platter or on individual plates. Place the chicken mixture on the leaves and sprinkle with mint leaves.

GRILLED CAPONATA
CHICKEN SALAD

The idea of grilling the vegetables for caponata comes from Johanne Killeen and George Germon, the proprietors of the wonderful Al Forno restaurant in Providence, Rhode Island. The concept forms the basis of this hearty dish, which makes for a perfect summer meal. Grilled bread rubbed with garlic and lightly brushed with good olive oil is all you need to add. ✖ *6 servings*

1 medium eggplant, unpeeled, cut into ½-inch-thick slices

2 large onions, red or sweet variety such as Vidalia or Bermuda, peeled and cut into ½-inch slices

½ cup (more or less) virgin olive oil

Salt

½ pound short, shaped pasta such as radiatore, penne, or cut ziti

1 small grilled or roasted chicken, boned and cut into large cubes

1 cup red or red and yellow cherry tomatoes, cut in half

¼ cup roughly chopped Italian parsley leaves

2 tablespoons fresh thyme leaves (optional)

1. Start a charcoal fire. When the coals are ready, lightly brush the eggplant and onion slices with olive oil and place on the grill rack to cook for 5 to 7 minutes on each side. Take care with this step; you want the vegetables to become lightly charred and cooked through. If the fire is too hot the vegetables will char too quickly on the outside and remain unpleasantly raw within. Remove the vegetables as they cook and set them aside.

2. Meanwhile, bring a medium-sized pot of water to a boil; add a pinch of salt and the pasta; cook until just al dente. Refresh the pasta immediately under cold water; drain well and turn into a large serving dish.

3. When they are cool enough to handle, place the grilled vegetables on a cutting board and cut them into cubes. Add the vegetables to the pasta. Add the chicken and the tomatoes and toss gently—try not to break up the vegetables too much. Sprinkle on the parsley and thyme and serve.

☛ **NOTE**: The grilled vegetables and tomatoes should exude enough of their own juices to make additional dressing unnecessary. However, if you feel the need, a small amount of olive oil or chicken broth can be added for additional moisture. A splash of red wine vinegar may be added in any case to brighten the flavors.

CHICKEN SALAD CAPRESE

*C*uprese is the name most often given to the widely popular Italian summer appetizer of tomatoes, mozzarella, and basil. Add chicken and a lively tomato vinaigrette—and a loaf of good bread—and you have the perfect warm weather meal. ✕ **6 servings**

3 whole poached or grilled chicken breasts, or the meat from a good-sized grilled or roasted chicken
1 pound fresh mozzarella cheese
3 large, excellent, ripe tomatoes
15 to 20 large basil leaves

DRESSING
1 medium ripe tomato, peeled, seeded, and cut into chunks
½ cup extra-virgin olive oil
1 garlic clove, peeled
10 large basil leaves
Salt
Freshly ground black pepper

1. Cut the chicken as well as you can into neat, flat slices. Cut the cheese and the tomato similarly, into approximately ¼-inch slices.

2. On a large serving platter, arrange the chicken, cheese, and tomatoes, alternating and overlapping them. Tuck basil leaves among the slices.

3. For the dressing, place the tomato and the olive oil in the work bowl of a food processor. Process to combine well. Drop the garlic and basil into the bowl and pulse or turn the machine on and off to chop the garlic and basil roughly into the dressing. Season with salt and freshly ground black pepper to taste. Drizzle the dressing over the salad, reserving some to pass at the table.

☛ **NOTE**: Acidity can vary from one tomato to another. If you think your dressing needs more, add a bit of red wine vinegar.

CHICKEN SALAD NIÇOISE

✖ *4 servings*

1 pound new potatoes or small all-purpose potatoes, unpeeled

¾ pound haricots verts or tender young green beans, trimmed

4 cups mixed tender lettuces, such as salad bowl, oakleaf, and frisée, washed and dried

2 whole poached chicken breasts, boned and skinned

4 hard-boiled eggs, peeled and quartered

3 medium ripe red tomatoes, quartered

3 scallions, trimmed, with about 2 inches green tops retained and thinly sliced

8 anchovy fillets, drained

DRESSING

1 cup extra-virgin olive oil

1 tablespoon red wine vinegar

1 tablespoon Dijon mustard

1 garlic clove, peeled

1 cup loosely packed basil leaves

Salt

Freshly ground black pepper

1. Bring a large pot of water to a boil. Add the potatoes and cook until tender; drain and refresh immediately in cold water. Drain again.

2. Bring another pot of water to a boil. Drop in the haricots verts and cook until just tender—2 to 3 minutes; take care not to overcook. Drain, refresh under cold water, and drain well.

3. To make the dressing, combine the oil, vinegar, mustard, and garlic in the work bowl of a food processor and process until smooth. Add the basil and pulse several times to chop it into the dressing. Season to taste with salt and pepper and additional vinegar if desired.

4. Toss the lettuces with about half the dressing in a large shallow bowl or deep platter. Cut the chicken into large chunks and arrange on the center of the lettuces. Cut the potatoes in half, or in quarters if they are not very small, and arrange them, the haricots verts, eggs, and tomatoes around the platter. Scatter the scallions over all and place the anchovies in a crisscross pattern over the chicken. Spoon on additional dressing and serve immediately (you may not need all the dressing).

PESTO GREEN BEANS AND PASTA CHICKEN SALAD

he idea for this comes from a recipe of Giuliano Bugialli. It has become one of my family's favorites. ✕ *6 to 8 servings*

Salt

½ pound short tubular pasta, such as penne or cut ziti, preferably whole wheat

1 pound haricots verts or fresh tender green beans, trimmed and washed

3 cups cubed broiled, grilled, or roasted chicken

• • • • • • • • • •

2 tablespoons pignolias (pine nuts), toasted

DRESSING

25 basil leaves

15 parsley leaves

¼ cup mayonnaise

3 tablespoons pignolias (pine nuts)

½ cup olive oil

2 garlic cloves, peeled

Salt

Freshly ground black pepper

1. Bring a large pot of water to a boil. Add a pinch of salt and the pasta and stir. When the pasta is cooked to within 2 or 3 minutes of the estimated time for al dente, drop in the haricots verts. Cook until the beans are just tender. Drain, refresh immediately under cold water, drain well, and turn into a large serving dish. Add the chicken to the dish.

2. Place the basil, parsley, mayonnaise, and pignolias into the work bowl of a food processor. Process to make a well blended, creamy mixture. With the machine running, pour the oil slowly through the food tube; blend well. Drop in the garlic and blend briefly. Season with salt and freshly ground black pepper to taste.

3. Pour the dressing over the salad ingredients in the bowl and toss to combine. Sprinkle with pignolias.

☛ **NOTE:** Two large ripe tomatoes, cut into wedges, are a nice garnish for this dish.

CHICKEN SALAD CAESAR

✖ *4 servings*

1 cup fresh white bread crumbs
½ cup freshly grated Parmesan cheese
Freshly ground white pepper
4 single chicken breasts, skinned, boned, and lighly pounded
1 egg, lightly beaten with 2 table-spoons water
About ½ cup olive oil for sautéing
2 garlic cloves, peeled and crushed
4 slices sturdy white bread, such as from a country or peasant loaf (if from a very large loaf, 2 slices cut in half)
2 large or 3 medium heads romaine lettuce

4 or more anchovy fillets, drained and chopped
Thin shavings of Parmesan cheese (optional)

DRESSING
⅓ cup olive oil or combination olive oil and other vegetable oil (but not corn oil)
1 tablespoon prepared Dijon mustard
1 tablespoon freshly squeezed lemon juice
Few dashes Tabasco or other red pepper sauce
1 egg boiled for 1 minute

1. Combine the bread crumbs, cheese, and white pepper on a large piece of wax paper. Dip the chicken breasts into the egg and then coat them with the bread crumb mixture.

2. Heat a large heavy skillet (cast-iron is ideal). Pour in just enough oil to cover the bottom of the skillet. Cook the breasts over medium-hot heat for about 3 minutes on each side; the crumbs should be golden brown and the breasts cooked through. Do not overcook. Remove the breasts to a platter lined with paper towels and set aside.

3. Wipe out the skillet and heat; again add oil to cover the bottom. Cook the garlic in the oil until golden brown; set aside. Quickly brown the bread on both sides in the oil and set aside.

4. Remove any tough or bruised outer leaves from the lettuce. Tear the rest into bite-sized pieces, omitting the ribs. Wash and dry the lettuce and place it in a large shallow salad bowl.

5. Whisk together the dressing ingredients. Pour the dressing over the lettuce and toss well.

6. Cut the chicken into large bite-sized pieces—about 2 inches—and arrange over the lettuce. Add the anchovies and Parmesan. Toss again at the table and place a slice of the sautéed bread topped with a bit of the garlic alongside each serving.

☛ **NOTE**: If you prefer the more traditional croutons, cut the sautéed bread into 1-inch cubes and toss into the salad with the chicken.

The chicken and bread can be prepared an hour or so in advance, but should not be refrigerated. Cut the chicken up just before adding it to the salad. The greens can be washed and the dressing prepared well in advance and kept in the refrigerator, but should be cool, not cold, when served.

MEDITERRANEAN CHICKEN SALAD

*nspiration for this comes from a recipe in Perla Meyers' **Art of Seasonal Cooking**. The preparation of the eggplant seems to keep it from absorbing too much oil, making it crisp and firm as a result.* ✘ *6 servings*

One 1-pound eggplant
2 red and 2 yellow bell peppers, or
    4 red peppers
2 ounces sun-dried tomatoes
¼ to ½ cup olive oil
Meat from one 3½-pound grilled
    or broiled chicken

DRESSING
1 to 2 tablespoons balsamic vinegar
⅓ cup extra-virgin olive oil
1 teaspoon red wine vinegar
1 garlic clove, peeled and minced
2 teaspoons fresh thyme leaves
Salt
Freshly ground black pepper

• • • • • • • • • •

2 bunches arugula or salad
    spinach, trimmed and washed

1. Cut the unpeeled eggplant into slices ¼ inch thick and then into ¼-inch-thick sticks. Place the eggplant in a large bowl and cover with ice water. Set aside for 1 hour.

2. Meanwhile, roast the peppers. Char them on all sides over the burners of a stove or under a broiler. Drop the peppers immediately into a plastic or paper bag and close. When the peppers are cool, peel off the skins. Cut the peppers in half and neatly cut away the seeds. Cut the peppers into ¼-inch-thick strips and set aside.

3. Place the sun-dried tomatoes in a small bowl and pour on just enough water to cover. Soak for 10 minutes, or longer if the tomatoes do not soften; drain. Pat the tomatoes dry and cut into slivers; set them aside.

4. After 1 hour, drain the eggplant; pat thoroughly dry with paper towels. Heat a large heavy skillet and pour in just enough olive oil to coat the bottom. Add the eggplant and cook, turning frequently, until the pieces are crisp and browned on all sides.

Add oil as needed. Do not crowd the pan; cook the eggplant in 2 batches if necessary.

5. Cut the chicken roughly into pieces that resemble the shape of the eggplant pieces. Place the chicken in a bowl along with the eggplant, peppers, and tomatoes. Whisk together the ingredients for the dressing, starting with 1 tablespoon of balsamic vinegar and adding more to taste; season with salt and freshly ground black pepper. Pour the dressing over the other ingredients ande gently toss to combine.

6. Arrange the arugula or spinach leaves on a serving platter and mound the salad in the center.

GAZPACHO CHICKEN SALAD

8 servings as appetizer, 6 servings as entrée

3 whole poached chicken breasts, boned, skinned, and separated

2 yellow or green (or one of each) bell peppers, trimmed of stems and seeds

2 cucumbers, peeled

1 small red onion, peeled

1 medium-sized jicama, peeled

DRESSING

¾ cup regular or low-fat sour cream

¾ cup low- or nonfat plain yogurt

⅓ cup snipped chives

1 jalapeño or other small hot pepper, trimmed of stem and seeds and minced

1 large garlic clove, peeled and minced

½ cup lime juice

3 medium-sized ripe tomatoes

1. Cut the breasts lengthwise into slices not more than ½ inch wide. Place the chicken in a mixing bowl.

2. Cut the peppers lengthwise into thin strips; add to the chicken.

3. Halve and seed the cucumbers; slice ¼-inch thick and add to the chicken.

4. Cut the onion in half and then lengthwise into thin slices; separate them, if necessary at the stem end. Add the onion to the bowl.

5. Cut the jicama into matchstick pieces and add them to the bowl.

6. Whisk together the dressing ingredients and pour over the vegetables. Toss to combine well.

7. Slice the tomatoes rather thickly, about ⅜ inch wide. Arrange the tomato slices on individual plates or in shallow soup plates. Mound the salad on the tomatoes and serve cold.

NOTE: Gazpacho, the soup, is sometimes garnished with garlic-flavored or herbed croutons, which could be included here as well. Or serve grilled or toasted bread brushed lightly with olive oil alongside.

EAST-WEST CARROT
CHICKEN SALAD

✖ *6 servings*

3 whole poached chicken breasts,
  boned and skinned

1 tablespoon light sesame oil

½ pound large shiitake mushrooms,
  stems removed, cut into ¼-inch
  slices

3 carrots, peeled, julienned, and
  cut in half crosswise

3 scallions, trimmed with about
  2 inches of green tops retained,
  julienned

1 large red bell pepper, trimmed,
  seeded, and julienned

1 jalapeño pepper, trimmed,
  seeded, and slivered lengthwise

¼ cup chicken broth

DRESSING

⅓ cup rice wine vinegar

⅔ cup light sesame oil

1 tablespoon dark sesame oil
  (optional)

1-inch piece fresh ginger, peeled
  and roughly chopped

1 garlic clove, peeled

½ cup loosely packed cilantro leaves

1. Shred the chicken, using your fingers; loosely cover and set aside.

2. Place a skillet or sauté pan over medium-high heat; add the sesame oil. Add the mushrooms and cook, stirring, for about 2 minutes; the mushrooms should be just softened and lightly browned.

3. Add the carrots, scallions, red pepper, jalapeño, and broth; turn the heat up to high, cover, and cook for about 1 minute, shaking the pan. This is just to soften the vegetables slightly. Remove from the heat and toss immediately with the shredded chicken.

4. Combine all the ingredients for the dressing in the work bowl of a food processor and whirl to combine well, but do not overblend. Toss the dressing with the chicken and vegetables and serve at once.

☛ **NOTE**: This is nice served in lettuce cups and accompanied by rice salad.

MID-EASTERN CHICKEN SALAD

✖ *8 servings as appetizer, 6 servings as entrée*

1 cup bulgur or cracked wheat

1 cup chopped Italian parsley
leaves

½ medium red onion, peeled and
chopped

4 scallions, trimmed, with 2 inches
green tops retained, sliced

2 small green peppers, trimmed of
stems and seeds, chopped

2 medium ripe tomatoes, peeled
and seeded, roughly chopped

½ cucumber, peeled, seeded, and
chopped

3 cups small-cube grilled or
broiled chicken

½ cup freshly squeezed lemon
juice

½ cup virgin olive oil

Inner leaves of 1 or 2 heads
romaine lettuce

¼ cup fresh mint leaves

20 or so oil-cured black olives

1. Place the wheat in a large bowl and cover with 4 cups of cold water. Soak for 20 minutes. Drain the wheat if any water has not been absorbed.

2. Add the parsley, onion, scallions, peppers, tomatoes, cucumber, and chicken to the wheat and mix well.

3. Whisk together the lemon juice and oil, pour over the wheat mixture, and combine thoroughly. Set the salad aside at cool room temperature for 3 to 4 hours.

4. Arrange the romaine leaves on a platter or on individual plates and mound the salad on top. Sprinkle with the mint leaves and garnish with the olives.

CHICKEN SALAD
FLORENTINE

Florentine" *is said to indicate the presence of spinach in a dish. That may be so, but to me, plump, luscious cannellini beans are as much a part of the traditional cooking of Florence, and indeed of much of Tuscany. It makes no difference here, since both spinach and cannellini beans are present in a salad that makes for a satisfying one-dish meal.* ✗*6 generous servings*

½ pound dried cannellini beans, soaked overnight

1 cup chicken broth

2 garlic cloves, smashed and peeled

2 whole fresh sage leaves

1 6- to 7-pound roasting chicken

1 head Roasted Garlic (page 29)

Freshly ground black pepper

Salt

3 or 4 large bunches fresh salad spinach, leaves torn from the ribs, washed, and dried (about 6 cups)

1. Drain the soaked beans and place them in a heavy medium-sized pot. Pour in the chicken broth and add enough water to cover by about 1½ inches; add the garlic cloves and sage leaves and a generous amount of pepper. Bring just to a boil, lower the heat, and simmer, covered, until the beans are tender but not mushy, 30 to 45 minutes (or even longer, depending on the age of the beans). Drain the beans, reserving the cooking liquid; discard the garlic and sage leaves. Return the cooking liquid to the pot, place over medium-high heat, and boil until the liquid is reduced to about ½ cup. Pour the reduced liquid into the work bowl of a food processor.

2. Meanwhile, roast the chicken according to the recipe on page 19. Remove the chicken from the roasting pan and pour the pan juices into a small bowl. Place the bowl in the refrigerator or freezer.

3. Remove the flesh from the roasted garlic and place it in the work bowl of the processor.

4. Remove and discard the fat that has risen to the surface of the chilled pan juices and place the defatted remaining juices into the work bowl with the bean liquid and garlic; process to blend. Taste and adjust the flavor with additional pepper and salt if needed. Add small amounts of broth if needed to achieve the texture of heavy cream.

5. Place the spinach in a deep platter or shallow bowl. Warm but do not boil the dressing and pour about half of it over the spinach. Toss the spinach quickly—it should wilt. Cut the meat from the roasted chicken in large pieces and arrange them over the spinach; place the beans among the chicken pieces. Drizzle a bit of the remaining dressing over the chicken and pass the rest at the table.

☛**NOTE:** The method given for removing the fat from the pan juices is the one that works best for me; if cold enough, the fat will solidify and leave behind dark, golden-brown, fat-free, and very tasty juices. You should use whatever method you favor.

WHEAT BERRY CHICKEN SALAD

✖6 to 8 servings

½ pound wheat berries
Salt
1 ounce dried porcini or other wild mushrooms
½ pound fresh mushrooms
1 tablespoon olive oil
½ cup chicken broth
4 or 5 slender leeks, trimmed, with about 1 inch green top retained
4 slender carrots, trimmed, peeled, and diced

3 whole poached chicken breasts, skinned, boned, and cubed
2 bunches salad spinach, trimmed, washed, and dried

DRESSING
1 teaspoon Dijon mustard
1 tablespoon sherry wine vinegar
½ cup hazelnut oil or light olive oil

1. Soak the wheat berries in water to cover generously for 15 minutes.

2. Bring a large pot of water to a boil; add a large pinch of salt. Drain the wheat berries and pour into the boiling water; lower the heat and simmer until the wheat berries are tender, 20 to 30 minutes. Drain and refresh under cold water. Drain and set aside.

3. Meanwhile, bring about 1 cup water to a boil. Pour the boiling water over the dried mushrooms. Soak the mushrooms for about 10 minutes; drain, straining and reserving the soaking liquid. Set the mushrooms aside.

4. Trim the fresh mushrooms and slice them about ¼ inch wide. Heat the olive oil in a medium-sized skillet over medium-high heat; add the mushrooms and toss briefly. Add ¼ cup of the broth and continue to cook until the mushrooms are lightly colored and the broth has been absorbed.

5. Slice the leeks crosswise about ¼ inch wide. Place the leeks in a colander and wash thoroughly; drain.

6. Place the remaining chicken broth in a covered skillet and bring to a simmer. Add the leeks and carrots, cover, and cook for 1 to 2 minutes to soften the vegetables slightly.

7. Place the wheat berries, both types of mushrooms, leeks, carrots, and chicken in a mixing bowl and toss to combine. Line a large shallow platter with spinach leaves.

8. Combine the dressing ingredients with 2 tablespoons of the reserved mushroom soaking liquid and whisk to combine well. Pour the dressing over the salad ingredients and toss well. Mound the salad in the center of the spinach leaves and serve.

WILD RICE CHICKEN SALAD

his is a wonderful lunch dish, or a first course especially in fall or winter. ✖8 to 10 servings as appetizer, 6 servings as entrée

8 ounces wild rice
⅓ cup cranberry juice or apple juice
⅓ cup dried currants
3 celery stalks, washed and trimmed
3 scallions, trimmed, including 1-inch green tops
3 whole poached chicken breasts, boned and skinned, cut into 1½-inch dice
1 cup red seedless grapes, or half red and half green, cut in half

Salt
Freshly ground white or black pepper

DRESSING
1 shallot, peeled and minced
¾ cup olive oil
2 or 3 tablespoons balsamic vinegar
1½ teaspoons fresh thyme leaves

• • • • • • • • • •

Leaves of radicchio or Boston lettuce

1. Cook the wild rice according to package directions until just tender. Drain and refresh under cold water. Drain and set aside.

2. Meanwhile, warm the juice, pour it over the currants, and leave for 5 to 10 minutes, to plump the currants. Drain the currants and reserve the soaking liquid.

3. Cut the celery stalks into thin crosswise slices.

4. Cut the scallions into thin crosswise slices.

5. Whisk together the dressing ingredients plus 1 tablespoon of the reserved currant soaking liquid.

6. Combine the rice, currants, celery, scallions, chicken, and grapes in a bowl.

7. Pour the dressing over the rice mixture and toss to combine; season to taste with salt and freshly ground white or black pepper.

8. Scoop the salad into individual lettuce cups or line a shallow bowl with the leaves and heap the salad in the center.

LENTILS AND CHICKEN SALAD

✕ 6 servings

½ pound lentils, preferably green
Salt
Small florets from 1 medium head broccoli
2 or 3 slender carrots, peeled and diced (about ½ cup)
3 cups cubed broiled, grilled, or roasted chicken

DRESSING
1 head Roasted Garlic (page 29)
¾ cup low- or nonfat plain yogurt
Juice of 1 lime
½ jalapeño or other small hot pepper, trimmed of stem and seeds
½ cup cilantro or parsley leaves

1. Bring a pot of water to a boil. Wash the lentils and add them to the pot; lower the heat and simmer until the lentils are just tender. The cooking time for lentils can vary dramatically, from 10 or 15 minutes to a half hour or more. Take care not to overcook them. Drain the lentils and refresh under cold water immediately; drain again and set aside.

2. Meanwhile, bring another pot of water to a boil; add a pinch of salt and the broccoli. Cook the broccoli just until al dente—2 to 3 minutes. Drain, refresh under cold water, drain well, and set aside.

3. Steam the carrots briefly, just to soften them slightly, or, if you prefer, leave them raw.

4. Place the roasted garlic cloves, the yogurt, and the lime juice in the work bowl of a food processor and blend well. Drop in the jalapeño and the cilantro and pulse or turn the machine on and off to chop them into the dressing; do not overblend.

5. Combine the lentils, broccoli, carrots, and chicken in a serving bowl. Pour on the dressing, toss to combine, and serve.

CHICKEN SALAD PANZANELLA

uscany's famous bread salad celebrates summer's best tomatoes and the inventiveness of frugal country cooks who do not let stale bread go to waste. This version, expanded with chicken, is inspired by the panzanella of my friend, cookbook author and teacher Giuliano Bugialli. There is no point making this with less than wonderful tomatoes. ✖6 to 8 servings

½ pound sturdy, heavy-crusted (but not sourdough) bread, preferably wholewheat, 2 to 3 days old, cut into large chunks

2 to 3 cups tepid water

¼ cup red wine vinegar

½ medium onion, peeled

½ large cucumber, peeled only if waxed

Inner heart of a head of celery, trimmed at the root end but with leaves retained

3 or 4 large ripe tomatoes

3½ to 4 cups large chunks grilled, broiled, or roasted chicken

10 to 12 large basil leaves

DRESSING

¾ cup extra-virgin olive oil

1 medium ripe tomato, peeled, seeded, and roughly cut up

1 large garlic clove, peeled

1 cup basil leaves, washed and dried

1. Place the bread in a large bowl. Combine the water and vinegar and pour over the bread; toss the bread to be sure the liquid is evenly distributed. Use enough water to moisten all the bread, but do not use more than is needed. Set aside for 2 hours or longer at room temperature.

2. Cut the onion into thin crosswise slices.

3. Cut the cucumber in half lengthwise, remove the seeds, and cut into ¼-inch crosswise slices.

4. Cut the celery into thin crosswise slices.

5. Cut the tomatoes into thick wedges and then cut the wedges in half crosswise.

6. Drain any excess water from the bread (there is unlikely to be any). Add the onion, celery, cucumber, tomatoes, and chicken to the bread and toss gently to combine.

7. Place the olive oil and the tomato in the work bowl of a food processor and blend well. Add the garlic and the basil and pulse or turn on and off to just chop the basil into the mixture; do not overblend.

8. Toss the bread mixture well with the dressing, garnish with the whole basil leaves, and serve.

☞ **NOTE:** The salad benefits from sitting at room temperature for an hour or so before serving.

CARIBBEAN CHICKEN SALAD

This reflects the tastes and styles of dishes that are found, variously interpreted, throughout the Caribbean islands.

6 servings

1 cup dried black-eyed peas, soaked overnight

Salt

1 cup long-grain rice

1 cup unsweetened coconut milk

1 cup chicken broth

1 red bell pepper, trimmed of stem and seeds and diced

1 green bell pepper, trimmed of stem and seeds and diced

¼ pound smoked ham, minced

Meat from 1 3½-pound grilled or broiled chicken, cubed

1 tablespoon turmeric

1 teaspoon chili powder

DRESSING

3 fresh or canned tomatillos

1 jalapeño or other small hot pepper, minced

1 garlic clove, peeled and minced

Scant ½ cup soy or light sesame oil

¼ cup white wine vinegar

1. Bring a medium-sized pot of water to a boil. Drain the peas and add them with a pinch of salt to the water. Cook the peas until just tender—15 to 30 minutes. Drain and refresh under cold water.

2. Meanwhile, place the rice in a pot and add the coconut milk and chicken broth; bring to a boil and add a pinch of salt. Turn the heat down, cover the pot, and simmer for 20 minutes. Spread the rice out on a sheet of aluminum foil to cool quickly without becoming gummy.

3. If using fresh tomatillos, remove the papery husks and bring a small pot of water to a boil. Drop in the tomatillos and cook at a low boil until tender, about 5 minutes; drain well. Mince the tomatillos and whisk them with the remaining ingredients for the dressing.

4. When the rice is cool, combine it with the peas, peppers, ham, and chicken in a serving dish and toss to combine; sprinkle on the turmeric and chili powder and toss again.

5. Pour on the dressing, toss to combine, and serve.

☞ **NOTE**: The coconut milk brings a creamy texture and subtle flavor to the rice, but if it is not available, an additional cup of chicken broth can be substituted.

SER MEOUN'S CAMBODIAN CHICKEN SALAD

er Meoun is one of the home cooks celebrated in Molly O'Neill's New York Cookbook, *which also serves as a guide to and history of the city's incredible food culture.* ✕ *4 to 6 servings*

½ bundle bean threads (cellophane noodles)

2 cups shredded cooked chicken

½ pound Chinese or Napa cabbage, shredded

1 carrot, peeled and shredded

1 cucumber, peeled, seeded, and shredded

1 small onion, peeled and thinly sliced

2 tablespoons chopped unsalted roasted peanuts

DRESSING

3 tablespoons nuoc nam (Asian fish sauce)

2 tablespoons rice wine vinegar

1 tablespoon sugar

2 garlic cloves, peeled and minced

• • • • • • • • •

2 tablespoons finely chopped fresh mint leaves

1. Bring a large pot of water to a boil; drop in the noodles and simmer for 2 minutes. Remove the pot from the heat and set aside until the noodles are tender, about 7 minutes. Drain the noodles and turn them into a large serving dish.

2. Add the chicken, cabbage, carrot, cucumber, and onion and toss to combine. Whisk together the ingredients for the dressing and pour it over the noodle mixture; toss again. Garnish with the mint leaves and peanuts and serve.

☞ **NOTE**: Bean threads and nuoc nam can be found in supermarkets that have good Asian food sections or in Asian markets.

CHICKEN SALAD SIRACUSA

✖ *6 servings as appetizer, 4 servings as entrée*

Salt

1 cup dried chick-peas, soaked in water overnight

3 medium all-purpose potatoes, or 6 new potatoes, washed but not peeled

⅓ cup golden raisins

½ cup chicken broth

4 cups cubed grilled, broiled, or roasted chicken

DRESSING

3 or 4 saffron threads

½ cup extra-virgin olive oil

2 teaspoons red wine vinegar

Salt

Freshly ground black pepper

· · · · · · · · · ·

¼ cup roughly chopped Italian parsley leaves

⅓ cup pignolias (pine nuts), toasted

6 to 10 green Sicilian olives, depending on size, the flesh cut away from the pits in pieces

1. Bring a large pot of water to a boil; add a large pinch salt. Drain the chick-peas and pour into the boiling water; lower the heat and simmer, partially covered, until the chick-peas are tender, 30 to 40 minutes. The time can vary, so begin testing after 20 minutes, and take care not to overcook. Drain and refresh the beans under cold water; set aside.

2. Bring another pot of water to a boil; add a pinch of salt and the potatoes. Cook the potatoes until just tender when pierced with a knife; do not overcook. Drain them and refresh immediately under cold water; drain and set aside.

3. Place the raisins in a small bowl. Warm the chicken broth and pour it over them; plump the raisins in the broth for about 5 minutes. Drain, reserving the soaking liquid.

4. Place the chick-peas, potatoes, raisins, and chicken in a serving bowl and toss gently to combine.

5. Warm ¼ cup of the reserved raisin soaking liquid; pour it over the saffron threads. Steep the threads for about 5 minutes and strain, reserving the liquid. Whisk the saffron liquid into the remaining dressing ingredients; season to taste with salt and freshly ground black pepper.

6. Pour the dressing over the salad ingredients and toss gently. Sprinkle on the parsley, pignolias and olive pieces, and serve.

OLIVE-FLAVORED CHICKEN-PASTA SALAD

✕ 6 generous servings

Salt
½ pound short pasta, such as radiatore, penne, or cut ziti
2 medium-sized sweet peppers, one red and one yellow if possible
2 tablespoons drained capers
Mcat from 1 3½-pound grilled or broiled chicken, cubed
½ cup roughly chopped basil

DRESSING
¼ cup commercial olive paste
2 tablespoons mayonnaise
Pinch hot red pepper flakes
1 or more tablespoons freshly squeezed lemon juice

1. Bring a large pot of water to a boil; add a pinch of salt and the pasta. Cook until al dente. Drain the pasta and refresh under cold water; drain well and turn into a serving dish.

2. Meanwhile, trim the peppers of their stems and seeds and cut lengthwise into thin slices. Add the peppers, capers, and chicken to the serving dish.

3. Whisk together the ingredients for the dressing; taste and adjust the flavors as necessary. Add the dressing to the salad and toss to combine. Sprinkle the basil over all and serve.

MEXICAN SALSA SALAD

✖ *6 servings*

½ pound pinto beans, soaked
   overnight
1 garlic clove, peeled and crushed
1 bay leaf
1 tablespoon cumin seeds
3 whole chicken breasts, boned,
   skinned, and separated
Kernels from 3 ears of corn
2 ripe avocados

MARINADE
¼ cup freshly squeezed lime juice
1 tablespoon ground chiles
1 tablespoon ground cumin seeds
2 tablespoons olive oil
1 tablespoon tomato paste

SALSA DRESSING
1 large ripe tomato
½ red onion, peeled and roughly
   cut up
1 jalapeño pepper, cut in half and
   trimmed of stem and seeds
½ cup cilantro leaves
1 teaspoon red wine vinegar
Salt
Freshly ground black pepper

• • • • • • • • • •

Good quality store-bought tortilla
   chips

1. Drain the beans and place them in a large pot; add the garlic, bay leaf, and cumin seeds. Cover by about 2 inches with cold water and bring to a boil over medium-high heat. Lower the heat, partially cover, and simmer until the beans are just tender, 20 to 30 minutes. Drain and refresh under cold water; discard the garlic and bay leaf. Drain well and place the beans in a large serving bowl or deep platter.

2. Place the chicken breasts in 1 layer in a glass or porcelain dish. Whisk together the marinade ingredients and coat each breast with the mixture. Cover the dish with plastic wrap and refrigerate for at least 6 hours or overnight.

3. Prepare a charcoal fire or heat the broiler. When the fire is ready, cook the breasts for 4 to 5 minutes on each side; they should be crisp and deeply colored on the outside and cooked through within. Set them aside for 15 minutes.

4. If the corn is very fresh and tender it may be used uncooked. If it is not, steam it for a minute or two in a covered skillet or in a microwave oven. Refresh under cold water, drain, and add to the beans.

5. Peel the avocados, cut them into 1½-inch chunks, and add to the beans and corn.

6. Cut each chicken breast down the middle and then across, into roughly 2-inch pieces. Add the chicken to the bowl.

7. Place the salsa ingredients in the work bowl of a food processor. Pulse or turn the machine on and off to make a rough mixture; taste and adjust the seasonings. Stir the salsa gently into the salad and toss carefully to combine. Serve, garnished with the tortilla chips.

GUMBO CHICKEN SALAD

✗ *6 to 8 servings*

½ pound large or jumbo shrimp in the shell
½ lemon, cut up
1 small bay leaf
Few dashes Tabasco or similar hot pepper sauce
6 peppercorns
1 cup long-grain rice
1 cup peas, fresh or frozen
3 cups cubed poached or roasted chicken
¼ pound baked ham, diced

DRESSING
¼ cup mayonnaise
¼ cup commercial Bloody Mary mix
Juice of ½ lemon
Tabasco or similar hot pepper sauce
Salt
Freshly ground pepper

1. Wash the shrimp and cut along the back; remove the vein, if any, but do not remove the shells. Place the lemon, bay leaf, Tabasco, and peppercorns in a medium-sized pot and add 2½ cups water. Bring to a simmer, cover, and simmer for 10 minutes. Add the shrimp and cook very briefly—2 to 3 minutes—just until cooked through. Drain, reserving the cooking liquid. Discard the lemon, bay leaf, and peppercorns and refresh the shrimp quickly under cold water; drain well and set aside.

2. Place the rice in the pot and pour in 2 cups of the reserved shrimp cooking liquid. Bring to a low boil over medium heat, lower the heat, cover, and simmer for about 20 minutes, until the rice is just done. Drain if there is excess liquid. Turn the rice onto a piece of aluminum foil or a large platter to cool quickly without becoming gummy.

3. If using fresh peas, steam them for 2 to 3 minutes in a covered small skillet or microwave oven, until just tender. Do not cook frozen peas.

4. Shell the shrimp and cut them in half if large and into 3 or 4 pieces if jumbo.

5. Combine the rice, peas, chicken, shrimp, and ham in a serving dish.

6. Whisk together the ingredients for the dressing. Taste and adjust seasonings, adding more lemon juice or Tabasco as needed. Add the dressing to the serving dish and toss well to combine. Taste again and season to taste with salt and freshly ground pepper.

☛ **NOTE:** My editor, Susan Friedland, recommends the following rice-cooking method, which she claims is foolproof (or gummy-proof): Simmer in a large quantity of water for 12 minutes; drain.

CHICKEN SALAD VERDE

✖ 6 to 8 servings

4 cups fresh spinach leaves,
  washed, tough leaves and ribs
  removed
Salt
½ pound farfalle (bowtie-shaped)
  or similar size pasta
1 pound sugar snap peas, trimmed
⅓ pound pancetta or slab bacon,
  cut into ¾-inch dice
2 teaspoons white wine vinegar

1 cup mayonnaise
1 tablespoon tarragon leaves
¼ cup Italian parsley leaves,
  washed and dried
3 whole poached chicken breasts,
  boned, skinned, and cut into
  1½- to 2-inch chunks, or about
  4 cups cubed roasted chicken

1. Steam the spinach leaves just until wilted, drain, and refresh immediately under cold water. Drain, gently squeeze out the excess water, and roll in paper towels. Set aside.

2. Bring a large pot of water to a boil, add a large pinch of salt, and add the pasta. When the pasta is about 2 minutes away from the estimated time for it to be cooked al dente, add the sugar snap peas. Cook just until the pasta and peas are al dente, pour into a colander, and refresh immediately under cold water. Drain well and pour into a large serving bowl.

3. Meanwhile, cook the pancetta or bacon in a small heavy skillet over medium heat until it is crisp and has given up most of its fat. Remove the pancetta with a slotted spoon and drain on paper towels; set aside.

4. Place the vinegar, mayonnaise, cooked spinach, tarragon, and parsley in the work bowl of a food processor. Pulse or turn on and off until the ingredients are well blended but not completely puréed—you should have a somewhat rough-textured thick mixture.

5. Pour the sauce over the pasta and sugar snaps and toss carefully to coat evenly. Add the chicken and toss again. Sprinkle the pancetta over all and serve immediately.

☛ **NOTE**: The various components can be prepared in advance and combined just before serving. If refrigerated, they should be brought to room temperature before serving.

BLACK BEANS AND RICE CHICKEN SALAD

✖ *8 servings*

1 cup dried black beans, soaked
  overnight
1 cup long-grain rice
1½ cups chicken broth
½ pound andouille sausage
1 medium onion, peeled and
  chopped
1 tablespoon olive oil
1 red pepper, trimmed of stem and
  seeds and chopped
1 green pepper, trimmed of stem
  and seeds and chopped
½ cup chopped celery
1 garlic clove, peeled and minced

3 whole chicken breasts, poached
  with one bay leaf and 3 or 4
  fresh thyme sprigs (or ½ teaspoon dried thyme) added to
  the poaching liquid

DRESSING
½ cup mayonnaise
¼ teaspoon cayenne
¼ teaspoon dried oregano
½ teaspoon dried thyme
Freshly ground pepper
1 teaspoon red wine vinegar
• • • • • • • • • •
¼ cup chopped parsley

1. Drain the beans, place them in a medium-sized pot, and cover by 2 inches with cold water. Bring to a low boil over medium-high heat; lower the heat, cover, and simmer until the beans are tender, 20 to 40 minutes. Drain the beans and refresh under cold water; drain well and set aside.

2. Place the rice in a medium pot; add 1 cup of the broth and 1 cup of water. Place the rice over medium-high heat and when it begins to boil, lower the heat, cover, and simmer for 20 minutes. Remove the rice from the heat and turn it out onto a piece of aluminum foil or a large platter to cool without becoming gummy.

3. Cut the sausage into ½-inch-wide diagonal slices. Place the sausage in a small skillet with ¼ cup of the remaining broth. Place the skillet over medium-high heat and steam the sausage for about 2 minutes, turning once. Remove from the heat and set aside.

4. Place the onion and the olive oil in the skillet and cook over medium heat for a minute or two, until the onion just begins to color slightly; do not burn it. Add the peppers, celery, garlic, and the remaining broth. Cover the skillet and cook the mixture over medium heat briefly, to just soften the vegetables slightly. Set aside.

5. Whisk together the ingredients for the dressing in a serving dish. Taste and adjust the seasonings. Add all the ingredients except the parsley and toss to combine; sprinkle on the parsley and serve.

☛ **NOTE:** If the cayenne, oregano, and thyme have been in your pantry for a long time, you may want to replace them to get enough flavor into this dressing. In any case, taste and adjust as noted.

SOUTHWESTERN CHICKEN SALAD

✕ *6 servings*

3 whole chicken breasts, boned, skinned, and separated
½ pound black beans, soaked overnight
1 bay leaf
1 large garlic clove, peeled and crushed
4 cups red and yellow cherry tomatoes, cut in half

MARINADE
Juice from 2 limes (¼ cup)
1 tablespoon olive oil
2 teaspoons chili powder
1 teaspoon ground cumin seeds

DRESSING
1 cup commercial cactus salsa
⅓ cup olive oil
1 tablespoon red wine vinegar
½ small red onion, peeled and roughly cut up
1 cup loosely packed cilantro leaves

• • • • • • • • •

Cilantro leaves
2 ripe avocados, peeled and sliced

1. Place the chicken breasts in 1 layer in a glass or porcelain dish. Whisk the ingredients for the marinade together and coat the breasts on both sides. Cover the dish with plastic wrap and refrigerate for at least 6 hours to overnight.

2. Drain the beans and place in a medium-sized pot. Pour in enough water to cover by 2 inches; add the bay leaf and garlic and place over medium-high heat. Bring to a low boil, lower the heat, and simmer, partially covered, until the beans are tender, 20 to 40 minutes. Do not overcook the beans. Drain and refresh under cold water and discard the bay leaf and garlic; drain well again.

3. Remove the chicken from the refrigerator about 15 minutes before cooking. Prepare a charcoal fire or heat the broiler (the fire is definitely preferable for this). When the fire is ready, cook the chicken for about 5 minutes on each side, until nicely browned and crisp on the outside and cooked through.

4. Combine the salsa, oil, vinegar, and onion in the work bowl of a food processor and pulse or turn on and off to make a coarse mixture. Add the cilantro and pulse briefly just to cut the cilantro into the dressing.

5. Combine the beans, tomatoes, and dressing in a bowl and stir to combine. Turn the mixture into a shallow bowl or deep platter. Cut each chicken breast on the diagonal into 3 or 4 pieces and arrange them in a row down the center of the bean mixture. Garnish with the cilantro leaves and the avocados.

☛ **NOTE:** Corn bread is good with this.

CHILLED JAPANESE BUCKWHEAT NOODLES AND CHICKEN

ere is another adaptation of a cold Japanese noodle dish. It is as good to eat as it is good for you. ✘ *4 servings*

¼ pound Japanese buckwheat noodles

Salt

4 dried shiitake or other Asian dried mushrooms

¼ cup chicken broth

2 tablespoons soy sauce

2 tablespoons sugar

2 whole raw chicken breasts, boned, skinned, and separated

1 tablespoon soy or light sesame oil

½ cup chopped scallions, white and green parts

2 tablespoons minced fresh ginger

1 bunch watercress, tender top stems and leaves only (about 2 cups)

DRESSING

½ cup rice wine vinegar

¼ cup soy sauce

2 teaspoons sugar

1 tablespoon freshly squeezed orange juice

• • • • • • • • • •

2 tablespoons lightly toasted sesame seeds

½ sheet nori seaweed, toasted and cut into 3-inch-long slivers (optional)

1. Bring a medium pot of water to a boil. Add the noodles and a pinch of salt. Cook the noodles until tender, about 10 minutes, then drain and refresh immediately under cold water. Drain well and set aside.

2. Meanwhile, soak the mushrooms in warm water to cover for 15 minutes; drain, squeeze out excess water, and slice into thin strips. Combine the chicken broth, soy sauce, and sugar in a small saucepan and bring to a simmer for 3 minutes; drain and set aside.

3. Using a very sharp knife, cut the chicken breasts into very thin slices.

4. Heat the oil in a 10-inch skillet over medium-high heat; add the scallions and ginger, then the chicken and the broth-soy sauce-sugar mixture, and sauté quickly, stirring constantly, until the chicken has lost its color, about 2 minutes. Remove the chicken from the pan and set aside.

5. In a serving dish, toss together the noodles, mushrooms, chicken, and watercress. Whisk together the ingredients for the dressing, pour over the noodle mixture, and toss well. Sprinkle the sesame seeds, then the nori slivers over all, and serve.

☞ **NOTE**: Both the buckwheat noodles and the nori can be found in Asian food shops and in many health food stores. Italian wholewheat noodles can be substituted for the buckwheat noodles.

CHICKEN SALAD "OSSOBUCO"

he flavors here come from the saffron-scented risotto that some-times accompanies Italian braised veal shanks, and the gremo-lata—a mix of lemon peel, parsley, and garlic—that flavors some versions. ✖ *8 servings as appetizer, 6 servings as entrée*

¾ cup long-grain rice
¾ cup chicken broth
3 or 4 saffron threads
¼ cup minced parsley
1 garlic clove, peeled and minced
Grated zest of 1 lemon
⅓ cup mayonnaise
2 whole poached chicken breasts, cubed

2 to 4 tablespoons chicken broth
Salt
Freshly ground white or black pepper
Unbruised leaves from 1 or 2 heads soft lettuce, such as Boston or Bibb, washed and dried

1. Place the rice in a medium-sized pot. Warm about ¼ cup of the chicken broth, pour it over the saffron, and steep for 3 minutes. Strain the liquid back into the remaining broth and discard the saffron. Add enough water to make 1½ cups liquid and pour it into the rice. Stir, and bring the rice to a low boil over medium-high heat. Lower the heat to a simmer, cover the pot, and cook for 17 to 18 minutes, or until you think the rice is about 2 minutes from being al dente. Quickly stir the parsley, garlic, and lemon zest into the rice, cover again, and cook until done.

2. Turn the rice out onto a platter or into a wide shallow bowl to cool quickly without becoming gummy. When the rice is cool, turn it into another bowl and stir in the mayonnaise. Add the chicken and combine well. Add the additional broth as needed to loosen the mixture. Season with salt and freshly ground white or black pepper to taste.

3. Arrange the lettuce leaves on a platter or on individual plates and heap the salad in the center.

I · N · D · E · X

I · N · D · E · X

L

Leeks, in wheat berry chicken
salad, 84

Lemon-chive "boiled" dressing,
Sara Belk's chicken salad
with, 36

Lentils and chicken salad, 87

M

Mangoes, in Zarela's ensalada
girasol, 48

Mayonnaise, 23–25
hard-boiled egg, 27

Mediterranean chicken
salad, 76

Mexican salsa salad, 94

Michael's grilled chicken and goat
cheese salad, 40

Mid-Eastern chicken salad, 81

Minced garlic chicken, Wolfgang
Puck's, 52

Mozzarella cheese, in chicken
salad Caprese, 71

Mushroom(s)
in artichoke chicken salad, 66
shiitake
in artichoke chicken salad,
66
in East-West chicken salad,
79
in wheat berry chicken salad, 84

N

New American chicken salad, 38

New Year's Eve chicken salad, 42

Noodles, somen, with chicken,
cold, 54

O

Old-fashioned chicken salad, 33

Olive(s)
in chicken tonnato, 47
-flavored chicken-pasta salad, 93

Onion(s)
in grilled caponata chicken
salad, 70

in Michael's grilled chicken

and goat cheese salad, 40

in Pacific Northwest chicken

salad, 49

in Wolfgang Puck's minced

garlic chicken, 52

Oranges, in chicken salad

Siciliana, 68

"Ossobucco," chicken salad, 106

P

Pacific Northwest chicken

salad, 49

Panzanella, chicken salad, 88

Parmesan cheese, in chicken salad

Caesar, 74

Parsley

in chicken tonnato, 47

in Mid-Eastern chicken

salad, 81

Pasta

and broccoli chicken salad, 57

in chicken salad verde, 98

and green beans chicken salad,

pesto, 73

in grilled caponata chicken

salad, 70

in Spring chicken salad, 64

Pears, in autumn chicken salad, 35

Peas

in gumbo chicken salad, 96

in Spring chicken salad, 64

Pepper(s), sweet bell

in black beans and rice chicken

salad, 100

in Caribbean chicken

salad, 90

in chicken salad "seviche," 45

in gazpacho chicken salad, 78

green, in Mid-Eastern chicken

salad, 81

in Mediterranean chicken

salad, 76

in Michael's grilled chicken

and goat cheese

salad, 40